Supporting Women after Domestic Violence

Supporting Women after Domestic Violence

Loss, Trauma and Recovery

Hilary Abrahams

Foreword by Cathy Humphreys

Jessica Kingsley Publishers
London and Philadelphia

First published in 2007
by Jessica Kingsley Publishers
116 Pentonville Road
London N1 9JB, UK
and
400 Market Street, Suite 400
Philadelphia, PA 19106, USA

www.jkp.com

Library of Congress Cataloging in Publication Data
Abrahams, Hilary, 1941-
   Supporting women after domestic violence : loss, trauma and recovery / Hilary Abrahams ; foreword by Cathy Humphreys.
      p. cm.
   Includes bibliographical references and index.
   ISBN-13: 978-1-84310-431-5 (pbk. : alk. paper) 1. Abused wives. 2. Marital violence. 3. Marital violence--Psychological aspects. 4. Psychological abuse. 5. Social networks. 6. Wife abuse--Prevention. I. Title.
   HV6626.A16 2007
   362.82'928--dc22

                                                    2007009912

British Library Cataloguing in Publication Data
A CIP catalogue record for this book is available from the British Library

ISBN 978 1 84310 431 5

Printed and bound in Great Britain by
Athenaeum Press, Gateshead, Tyne and Wear

08 08

In memory of my mother, Dorothy,
for whom there was never any refuge

Acknowledgements

This book was made possible through the interest, involvement and support of many women. My thanks go to:

- the residents and former residents of Penzance, Birmingham and York Women's Aid refuges, who were willing to share their experiences and thoughts to establish a better understanding of their issues and support needs and to help other women

- the workers, volunteer staff and management at the refuges who took time out of their busy lives to explain, advise, discuss and comment

- all the members of Women's Aid who have helped in shaping the research on which this book is based with their ideas, comments and feedback

- my advisors, Ellen Malos and Nicola Harwin, and my support group, especially Emma, Judith, Louise and Mandy

- and finally to Ian, for his unfailing support and encouragement.

Contents

Figures

Table

Foreword

Domestic violence corrodes the fabric of women's emotional and social worlds. The process of extinguishing a woman's sense of herself, her relationships, her understanding of her past and her present is a destructive one. It occurs behind closed doors and thrives in an environment of secrecy and isolation. Unsurprisingly, others, including professionals have had little access to this closed world and its destructive interior.

Paradoxically, the route to safety has also, and by necessity, often occurred behind closed doors. There has been little exposure of the complex process of support and healing which has been undertaken with workers and other women within the refuge sector. The need for secret addresses, high levels of security, and privacy to allow the slow process of recovery has meant that the work of refuges has also been subject to invisibility.

This book brings to light the complexity of this work and women's journeys. It is not before time. The context of women's services is changing. The entwining of advocacy for services combined with the high levels of emotional support required for women to embark on the difficult pathway to recovery is changing – and not always for the best. A number of challenges beset both individual women and the sector.

Firstly, the drive to provide cheaper and more 'efficient' accommodation for women and children escaping domestic violence has frequently meant that the complex array of services provided through refuges has been underestimated. The threat to specialist refuges for black and minority ethnic women, and the drive to provide only minimal support through hostel accommodation fails to recognise the level of fear, trauma and grief which the crisis of separation can represent. It is not a time to leave women alone to fend for themselves when this act of independence and bravery can provide the first step towards a new life free from violence. High level support is essential and cost effective and should not be constructed as a luxury. This book provides a graphic reminder that this is the case.

The second issue lies in contrast, and possibly contradiction to the first. This is namely that domestic violence intervention is becoming increasingly professionalised. Domestic violence forums are dominated by police, health professionals, social workers and housing workers. While this mainstreaming is an exciting development which can create significantly more attention to domestic violence, it carries with it some dangers. These can include downgrading the high levels of competence and experience provided by Women's Aid and other specialist voluntary sector organisations, as well as an underestimation of the role and value of mutual support provided by one survivor towards another and the effectiveness of creating shared activities for children.

Understanding the balance to be struck is particularly evident when the intervention to support the emotional well-being of both women and children is considered. Recognition that the impact of violence and abuse can be traumatising and that the erosion of women's esteem and identity can lead to depression, high anxiety and suicide attempts is not new. However, problems arise if we then think that only professional counsellors and mental health professionals are able to provide the requisite help. Again, this book provides an important reminder that mutual support should be considered a central rather than a peripheral aspect of the healing journey for many women. The interviews with women in refuges provide testimony to its significance and a reminder that as the 'purpose built refuge' characterised by separate accommodation units for women and children emerges, that steps are required by workers to facilitate the opportunities for women to get to know and support each other in their day- to-day living. A major step in the recovery from trauma and hence recovery in the aftermath of violence is to re-establish social support and step away from the isolation created by violence and abuse.

A book which traces the patterns in the journeys towards recovery for women escaping violence simultaneously highlights the extraordinary nature of this journey and, paradoxically its essential grounding in the ordinary – the everyday. Reclaiming a life in which daily relationships are not embedded with fear is part of this journey. The graphic stories in this book highlight this important message. It draws our attention to the role of safety in providing an underpinning for the road to recovery, one which is paved by the entwining of professional support with that of the everyday support which can be given by one woman to another. Opening the door on the practices in refuges which provide the context for this ordinary, yet often extraordinary experience, it is compelling reading for anyone working with women and children living with and leaving domestic violence.

Cathy Humphreys
Alfred Felton Chair in Child and Family Welfare,
University of Melbourne Victoria, Australia

Introduction

At the heart of a situation of domestic violence is one individual, most often a woman, who is paying a heavy personal, social, economic and emotional cost. She may have children – or not. She may be married – or not. She may have learning difficulties or physical impairments, be old or young, a member of a religious, ethnic or cultural minority or of any class of society. For any woman who is in a violent relationship, seeking to leave it, or trying to find the strength to rebuild her life after doing so, there is a need not only for practical support to enable her to access appropriate services, but also for emotional support to build up shattered confidence and self-esteem. For some women, this support may be needed for a relatively short period; for others it may need to extend over a much longer timescale.

This book explores the nature of these support needs, drawing on the experiences of women who have left an abusive relationship and stayed for a time in refuges run by members of the Women's Aid Federation of England. It reveals a complex picture of practical and emotional requirements and responses and the importance of a network of internal and external support resources which women can draw on, both during the refuge stay and afterwards. Women and workers discuss the difficulties and conflicts which can hold women back, the factors that they regarded as crucial in providing effective support and the need for an holistic approach which respects the individual and her concerns.

From these insights has emerged a new way of understanding the impact of domestic violence and abuse[1] on emotional health and the ability to recover. This approach, which uses Maslow's ideas[2] on human needs, acknowledges the positive agency of the woman herself and gives full value to the contribution which can be made by a supportive community. At the same time, the process of leaving the relationship and eventual reintegration into a new community is shown as being similar to the pattern of rebuilding a life following bereavement. Taken together, these two perspectives offer a model of loss and recovery: the loss made more traumatic by the effects of domestic violence on confidence and self-esteem. This model creates a framework of understanding that can assist agencies and organisations to recognise the nature of the emotional as well as practical difficulties which women face, and to provide appropriate and cost-effective services. For women who are experiencing, or have experienced, domestic violence,[3] it offers a way of making sense of events and feelings that can seem bewildering and chaotic, enabling them to locate themselves in a process with an ending and to recognise their own capabilities of taking action and influencing outcomes.

Although the women who participated in this study had been, or were, resident in refuges, the concepts involved have implications not simply for all those associated with the provision of refuge or hostel accommodation, but for other freestanding support services in the community, including outreach support, community groups and advocacy services and for a wide range of professional organisations and agencies whose work brings them into contact with aspects of domestic violence, including social workers, health professionals, counsellors, teachers and housing officers. Nor is this intended to be limited to work with women; men, too, can be subject to violence and abuse from intimates and an understanding and appreciation of its impact and the process of recovery can be used to inform support work in this area.

About the project

The research on which this book is based was carried out as a collaborative project with the Women's Aid Federation of England, and in particular with three of its member groups based in Penzance, Birmingham and York. The federation, and its sister organisations in Wales, Scotland and Northern Ireland, have built up a network of services since the 1970s that has become recognised as a major source of advice, information, support and safe accommodation for women experiencing domestic violence. The values and approach that inform the work of its members and are reflected in the chapters which follow are detailed in Appendix 1.

A total of 23 women, whose ages ranged from 21 to 68, took part in the study. Some were still in a refuge; others had been living independently for up to five years. Although they came from a wide range of geographical, socioeconomic, educational and cultural backgrounds and were currently living in a range of different environments, there was remarkable unanimity in what they praised and what they criticised; their accounts of the stresses and emotional difficulties they faced; the factors they saw as important and what they wanted in terms of support services. General refuge workers, volunteers, outreach and helpline staff, children's workers and counsellors, together with managers and administrators, also took part in the research, discussing their approach to supporting women and the challenges they faced in providing effective services. Further details of the research methods, the ethical considerations involved and of the participants can be found in Appendix 2. A guide to the issues covered in the research is detailed in Appendix 3.

About the book

Chapter 1 offers a base definition of domestic violence, a broad outline of the range and scope of acts which can be involved, the effects on physical and mental health and the social and economic deprivation it can cause. Women describe the impact of the abuse on their lives and, in particular, on their emotional well-being and personal integrity. Using Maslow's ideas on human need, I suggest that these effects can be seen as reducing an individual's concerns and outlook down to the primal needs of survival, making it immensely difficult to leave the relationship and to commence the process of rebuilding confidence and the capacity for independent action. These effects can also be interpreted as forming the evidence for a diagnosis of post traumatic stress disorder (PTSD) and I discuss the implications of this, arguing that, although the use of this term can be advantageous for some women, there can be adverse social and economic consequences for others. For the majority of women, the use of Maslow's ideas offers an alternative, non-stigmatising approach, while retaining the availability of a medical interpretation to enable those women who require it to seek assistance from mental health professionals. Finally, the chapter examines the impact of the losses, both in emotional and material terms, which are imposed by domestic violence and how women who manage to leave the relationship come to terms with this, begin to recover from the abuse and construct a new life for themselves, drawing out the similarities between this process and that generally recognised as following bereavement.

The next four chapters trace in more detail the personal journey of recovery being made by the women who talked to me. Chapter 2 recounts the (sometimes surprising) ways in which women learnt of the availability of safe accommodation and support and the factors that were involved in making the decision to leave. It looks at their arrival at the refuge, the practical and emotional support that was needed at this time and their reactions to the refuge, the workers and other residents.

Chapter 3 takes the journey a stage further, examining the way in which support needs changed following the initial impact of leaving, the growth of trust and empowerment and the use of advocacy and counselling skills in the provision of support. It explores the fluid and dynamic nature of change and growth, the intense emotional stresses involved and the difficult task for workers in maintaining a balance between support and dependency.

Chapter 4 steps back a little from this journey, looking at the ways in which women sought to reconnect to others and end the isolation imposed on them by their abuser, the normalising power of everyday conversation, contact with workers and the use made of other forms of communication, including counselling, formal and informal group work, and activities such as life skills training and outings.

In Chapter 5 women discuss the benefits and disadvantages of communal living, their reactions to conflict and tension within the refuge and put forward their ideas on what is most needed in this type of accommodation.

Chapter 6 takes us beyond the refuge and into the next stage of the journey: rehousing, the continuing need for longer term practical and emotional support and the importance of knowing that there is a community which would be 'there for them' if needed. It also looks at the way in which some women had developed a radically changed sense of their own identity and their role in society since leaving the relationship and how this had affected their subsequent life choices.

In Chapter 7, the concepts, attitudes and approaches featured in the previous chapters are brought together and discussed in more detail. The six elements that women unanimously selected as being fundamental in assisting them to rebuild their lives are examined. These six factors – physical and mental safety, respect, a non-judgemental approach, being believed, time to talk and be heard and mutual support – characterised effective support giving and were seen as crucial in a successful transition to independent living. This chapter also discusses the role of the refuge workers, the approach they took to their work and their needs for support to enable then to work effectively with women in a stressed and pressurised environment.

Chapter 8 brings together the various strands covered by the research on which this book was based and relates them to the concepts discussed in Chapter 1 to show how the concept of recovery from immense loss, made more complex and difficult by the effects of domestic violence, can be used to inform service provision in a wide range of settings and help women to make sense of their experiences and understand their own capacity to act for themselves. It also examines the wider implications of the research, its application to other situations of domestic abuse, including female/male violence, same-sex relationships and family violence and how the concepts it identifies can be used in working with individuals who are still in an abusive relationship.

To leave a relationship and enter a refuge is, as will be seen from the stories of my informants, a hard choice to make. It was only after having made that decision that they became fully aware that this was just the start of a long process of rebuilding both their physical lives and their emotional capabilities. It is, as Liz[4] explained to me, 'a long, hard road to go by'. This research attempts to give some shape to a journey that can often seem fragmented and uncertain and to offer some milestones along the way.

Notes

1.   Domestic violence is the term most commonly used in the UK to describe a range of violent and abusive behaviours. A fuller definition is given in Chapter 2.

2.   Maslow (1987, first published 1954).

3.   Considerable debate has taken place both within the domestic violence field and at policy level, around the use of the terms 'victim' and 'survivor' (Kirkwood 1993; Skinner 1999; Williamson 1999). The women who talked to me saw themselves first and foremost as individuals with their own views on who and what they were – views which might change from day to day. In line with their expressed views, the term 'women who experience domestic violence' has been adopted for use throughout the book.

4.   Names of women, workers and volunteers have been changed to preserve anonymity and confidentiality and no reference is made as to which refuge they worked in, or had been accommodated in.

Chapter 1

Why Doesn't She Just Leave?

It was evident from their accounts that most of the women who talked to me had experienced abuse for between five and ten years. For some, it had extended over a much longer period – one woman had suffered emotional abuse for almost 40 years. It can be difficult, not only for the general public, but also for some professionals who come in contact with them, to understand why women remain in these relationships; or, if they leave, why they are likely to return to their abuser on one or more occasions. This may lead to feelings of frustration and perhaps the view that there is little point in taking action in the case under consideration, or indeed in subsequent similar cases.[1] For the woman who is experiencing domestic violence, there are complex issues around staying, leaving or returning. Some of these may revolve around the relationship itself, where feelings may be confused, ambiguous and painful. Others may relate to the practicalities of leaving – the losses that will be sustained in the process, access to material resources and support, loneliness, having to manage alone, the needs of her children and the fear of retribution. Underlying all of this will be the effects that domestic violence have had on her physical health and mental and emotional well-being.

The effects of domestic violence

Over the past decade, many definitions of domestic violence have been adopted by agencies and organisations working in this field. To enable a base to be established for data collection and information sharing, the government has agreed a common, core definition for use across all departments which can also be adopted by local domestic violence partnerships. This states that domestic violence is:

> Any incident of threatening behaviour, violence or abuse (psychological, physical, sexual, financial or emotional) between adults who are or have been intimate partners or family members, regardless of gender[2] or sexuality. (Home Office 2004)

The majority of partnerships move to develop fuller definitions, which maintain compatibility with the core definition, while reflecting the realities of their own situations, their remit and their aims and objectives. But what does this definition mean in reality? Table 1.1 lists some of the ways domestic violence can be manifested.

Table 1.1 Examples of domestic violence	
Mental abuse	**Physical Violence**
• Threats • Fear • Threat to harm children • Isolation from family and friends • Loss of social contact • Persistent criticism • Denial of privacy • Verbal abuse • Deprived of sleep, money, clothes, going out, use of telephone • Terror and intimidation	• Throwing things • Kicking, slapping, hitting • Pushing, shoving, grabbing • Choking, strangling, suffocating • Using a weapon • Bruising, broken bones, cuts, scratches • Bitten, burnt, scalded • Knocking unconscious • Miscarriage due to violence • Chemical in face • Death
Sexual violence	**Other forms of abuse**
• Rape • Sexual assault • Degrading and humiliating sexual acts	• Damage to personal property • Theft of property • Threats and violence to pets, animals • Denied access to work

This is by no means an inclusive or definitive list, but is intended to show some of the many different ways in which abuse can take place and has been compiled from research carried out over the past ten years. Sources include Dobash *et al.* (2000), Glass (1995), Kirkwood (1993), Mirrlees-Black (1999), Mooney (2000), Stanko *et al.* (1998).

Physical or sexual violence is not usually confined to a single episode – repeated incidents, which increase in frequency and intensity over time, are the most common pattern.[3] Once the first physical or sexual incident, however minor, has taken place, there will inevitably be the anticipation and fear of further violence, resulting in growing feelings of anxiety and uncertainty. Other forms of abuse – constant criticism and belittling, possessive and controlling behaviour, isolation, access to money and other resources – may be combined with physical or sexual abuse, or be used alone, but equally create feelings of anticipatory fear and anxiety. Women explained that they were constantly wondering and worrying as to what their partner's mood was going to be. Would it be a quiet, peaceful day with just a few plates thrown, or would it start badly and get much, much worse? The unpredictable nature and timing of the abuse removed from them any sense of physical or mental safety. As a result they were unable ever to be at ease, or to trust what was going on around them.

Acts of physical and sexual violence had often severely injured them and some women had suffered permanent damage to their physical health. Yet they were emphatic that it had been the mental consequences of these acts and of the other emotional abuse that they had suffered – the 'mind games', manipulation and control which their abusers attempted to exercise over every aspect of their lives and thoughts – that had been the hardest to bear. It was in some ways, they told me, worse than the physical abuse, since they were unable to show evidence of the damage that had been caused to their emotional well-being and mental health and from which they felt they might never recover. 'He just messed with my head so much' was a frequent comment. This stress on the psychological impact of abuse has been noted by other researchers in this field.[4]

Women talked about the way their world had 'closed in' as they became isolated by their abuser from communication with family and friends, either through direct prohibition, or by making it extremely difficult to maintain contact. For example, the amount of money available for transport might be restricted, or aggressive and insulting behaviour might drive away those who came to visit. Some women, perhaps with elderly or infirm relatives, did not want to expose them to the risk of abuse. There were also feelings of shame and guilt around what was happening, which could make them reluctant to make contact. Their connections with the wider community were also subject to control and scrutiny. Shopping trips were timed and closely monitored, with lengthy interrogations as to whom they had met and talked to and any activities outside the home were implicitly or explicitly discouraged. (In one case, this included regular hospital check-ups to monitor medication levels.) This isolation was made worse in rural areas by lack of adequate public transport and accessible community facilities. Some women had been forbidden to use the telephone, or it had been ripped out. Jobs had also been given up or lost because of the level of control exercised over outside contacts, taking away access to independent financial resources, as well as social contact with workmates. The same had been true of further education, or other study.

With the diminution of potentially supportive networks, communication with the only permitted source of conversation, the abuser, became more significant, influencing women's views on life in general and in particular, their view of themselves. Inevitably, this had a negative effect, with women like Stacey talking of the effect that constant criticism of their appearance, intelligence and ability had had on them. 'The emotional abuse is terrible. To be told, for nearly eight years, that I was stupid and I was thick and…you know, you believe it.'

Perhaps the saddest, yet most tenuous aspect of this emotional abuse was the way in which it appeared to have destroyed women's own aspirations and ideals. This was most poignantly expressed in two lines of a poem that Amalie had written while in the refuge and showed to me:

> He took my hopes and my dreams
> And my reach for the stars.

Isolation and constant denigration resulted in a gradual and terrifying erosion of their personal integrity – of being a person in their own right, with ideas and ideals worthy of recognition and respect. They lost confidence in themselves and their abilities, their self-respect and self-esteem, feeling, as they had been told so often, that they were 'worthless' and 'a waste of space'.

No one aspect of abuse can be seen as standing alone – they feed on each other. Physical and emotional abuses both create an atmosphere of fear, shame, uncertainty and lack of trust that places a barrier between women and those around them, isolating them from potential sources of support. Possessive and controlling behaviour results in economic and social deprivation by limiting access to clothes and other material goods, transport, education and social activities, further increasing feelings of isolation and reinforcing the dominance and importance of the abuser. Without outside support to check the reality of her perceptions, isolation turns thoughts inward to review what is happening, resulting in an inversion of reality, whereby the woman believes that she is the one to blame. Her sense of guilt and shame works to increase her isolation and ability to trust herself or those around her. Amy described how this happened to her:

> Because you are isolated, you're going through it, you are isolated, because you are blaming yourself all the time. You see the man as the good one. Yeah, he's right. In the end, you've got no…you know, you seem so down you think, well, it *is* all my fault. So, in the end, you're scared to talk to anyone. And I found myself thinking, they all know. They all know that… They all think that it's my fault.

Consequently, women are held in an abusive relationship by what has aptly been termed a 'web'[5] of interrelated behaviours and social and economic difficulties; by both fear and the reality which reinforces it.

It takes courage and determination just to keep going in these circumstances, let alone take the decision to leave. It was clear, however, that women did take positive action to protect themselves and their children and to maintain some kind of contact with other people. They made efforts to defuse tension in potentially dangerous situations, trying to please and satisfy the abuser, monitoring their own behaviour to avoid confrontation and looking for ways out of their situation, including leaving temporarily to give themselves respite and time to think. They had utilised helplines, either by using mobile phones or, where they were allowed unchecked access, by landlines. They used drop-in centres, did their best to keep the home together and took whatever opportunities offered to be in contact with others. Those who had jobs tried hard to keep them, and if they lost them looked for other paid or voluntary positions.[6] These strategies contrast strongly with the idea of 'learned helplessness' (Walker 1984), a concept which argues that women who experience repeated abuse become helpless, passive and submissive, feeling powerless to control their lives and unable to leave the relationship. In her later work, Walker (1993) has modified this concept to accept that the overall position is more complex. Women are not totally helpless or passive within an individual incident or continuing situation. Nevertheless, 'learned helplessness' has been widely adopted by social workers, the medical profession and other agencies[7] and can result in the woman being seen as 'the problem' rather than the abuser.

A framework for understanding

An appreciation of the overall effects of domestic violence and a way of understanding the sort of support needed by those who experience it can be gained by considering them in relation to Maslow's ideas on human needs, first published in 1954 (Figure 1.1). As a psychologist, Maslow saw human need, not simply as the requirement for food, water, shelter and clothing in order to maintain existence, but as a deeper drive within individuals to create for themselves an adequate and fulfilling life and to reach out for those elements which they felt were lacking in their present circumstances. He argued that people have higher needs and aspirations. Once the basic physiological needs for survival had been at least partially met, they would want to reach beyond these to achieve some measure of safety and freedom from fear, to belong, to connect to others and be accepted by them, to experience feelings of self-worth and self-esteem and to develop their own ideals and abilities. He saw individuals as actively seeking to meet their needs as they perceived them and to care for themselves in whatever way they felt was appropriate: for example, that they would seek safety before looking for the esteem of others. He also argued that the innate ability to do this might be limited by the social and economic circumstances in which they lived and their past and current experiences, which had the capacity to damage or block their capability of taking action.

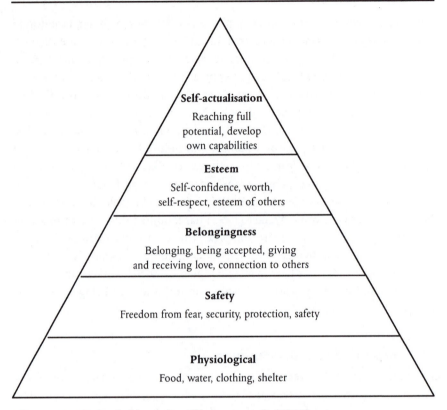

Figure 1.1 Maslow's hierarchy of human needs (1987)

Interpreting these ideas in terms of the effects of domestic violence, the experiences of the women in this study show that the physical and, in particular, the mental abuse they had suffered, with its uncertainty and the unpredictability of its occurrences, had removed any sense of physical or mental safety and security. The feelings of fear and shame that this induced deterred women from confiding in those around them and this isolation from others was further reinforced by mechanisms of control and coercion. Over time, they had lost confidence in themselves and their sense of worth and self-esteem, accepting the value placed upon them by their abuser and losing their own aspirations (the 'reach for the stars' yearning voiced by Amalie). This in turn reinforced isolation and fear, leaving women with only the basic drive to survive and maintain life for themselves and their children.

Yet, at the same time, they were taking positive action, as Maslow envisaged, caring for themselves, as far as they could, in terms of safety and, where it could be done without increasing the risk to themselves or others, reaching out and making connections. Safety was also an important consideration in deciding to leave or stay in the relationship. For many women, leaving may be the more dangerous option. They expressed considerable fears as to what would happen if they were located by their abuser. 'If he finds me, I'm dead' was one blunt and probably realistic assessment of the situation, bearing in mind that official statistics show that two women a week are killed by partners or former partners, a figure which has not altered for more than a decade (Povey 2004). Research also suggests that women may be at the greatest risk of harm when they are seeking help, or are at the point of leaving the relationship (Mullender and Morley 1994).

Seeing the effects of domestic violence in this way may make it easier to appreciate the extent and the interlinked nature of the difficulties that a woman who experiences domestic violence has to contend with and the factors which may influence her choices and decision-making processes. In terms of Maslow's ideas, effective support for women who experience domestic violence needs to recognise and reinforce their own ability to take action. It needs to establish a sense of a physically and mentally safe space, to provide a supportive environment where a woman can feel believed and accepted by others and to work with her to rebuild the confidence and self-esteem which will enable her to regain autonomy and control over her life. Support also needs to be reliable and consistent, to avoid increasing any feelings of isolation, or of not being 'worthy' of support and may be needed over a considerable period of time. A recent study of a number of intervention projects by Hester and Westmarland (2005) has shown that these are all the factors most valued by service users and seen by workers as most effective in offering successful support.

This support may come from a variety of sources: from community projects such as 'one-stop-shops'; the outreach and support services run by refuge groups and other voluntary organisations; and from advocacy and health initiatives. National and local helplines also have an important role to play both in providing immediate contact and in putting women in touch with other sources of help. Support need not be seen as limited only to specific organisations. It can be crucially important when offered by individuals who may come in contact with the woman or her family in a variety of settings, including education, employment and health. Nor does it need an official position – the everyday contacts which women made with others – at the school gates, for example – were valued as sources of support and 'normality'.

Post traumatic stress disorder

Research has shown clear links between women's experience of domestic abuse and a range of mental health problems, including depression, post traumatic stress disorder (PTSD) self-harming behaviours and suicidality.[8]

PTSD was originally seen as a consequence of the experiences of combat troops, but has now been recognised as affecting hostages and the victims and witnesses of major disasters. It has also, thanks to the efforts of feminists working professionally in the mental health field (Dutton 1992; Herman 1992), been extended to include individuals who experience rape and sexual abuse as adults or children and those who experience domestic violence, where the long-term nature of much of this abuse makes it more complex and traumatic than a single incident. It is the parallel with the hostage scenario that is particularly relevant to women who experience domestic violence, since they, like hostages, exist in a situation where unpredictable events remove any sense of physical and mental safety. They are isolated from any source of contact except the hostage taker or takers and lose confidence in themselves, their own identity and sense of self-worth, seeking only to survive the experience. Guidance on supporting recovery from PTSD stresses that the first consideration must be the establishment of physical and mental safety in a supportive atmosphere, the rebuilding of self-esteem and autonomy, and links to family, friends, community and wider society.

The advantage of a diagnosis of PTSD is that it directly links domestic violence with its effects on mental health and emotional well-being and can enable a woman to access professional help, including appropriate medication, without feeling that she is, in some respect, personally deficient, inferior or inadequate, as might be the case with a diagnosis such as 'borderline personality disorder'. However, it can be seen as continuing to pathologise women, focusing on 'the woman' and 'her problem' rather than taking account of the situation that has caused it, the controlling nature of the abuse and the circumstances in which she may have to continue to live. Diagnoses of this nature are made by mental health professionals, and as Dutton (1992) and Whalen (1996) have pointed out, the power for recovery may then be seen to lie with the professional counsellor or psychotherapist and become medicalised, rather than rest with the individual woman and the sources of support that she chooses.[9] For the woman herself and those around her, such a diagnosis can be seen as a stigma. It may disadvantage her in dealing with potential employers and with professional and statutory bodies. This may also be the case, as Humphreys and Thiara (2003) point out, within the legal system, in matters such as child contact cases or residence orders.

Although a diagnosis of PTSD can be extremely valuable in enabling the comparatively small number of women who require or can access it, to obtain specialist help, it would seem to be inappropriate as a blanket diagnosis for all women who experience domestic violence. The women who talked to me were well aware of the immense effect that psychological abuse had had on them and were concerned about the problems that this created for them in their efforts to move on. All of them displayed, to a greater or lesser degree, symptoms associated with PTSD, but none of them saw themselves as needing to access professional mental health services or specialist trauma interventions. To see their experiences in terms of Maslow's ideas, however, provides an alternative approach which mirrors the concepts involved in the diagnosis and treatment associated with PTSD, but can be seen as more appropriate for the majority of women who experience domestic violence. It removes any concept of stigma, pathology or 'victim blaming' and conveys a positive and accurate image of women actively striving to overcome difficult personal circumstances, enduring social and economic disadvantage and reacting in an understandable way to what they have been through. This approach both recognises the important role of networks and communities in recovery and adds a spiritual dimension in recognising the importance of higher values and personal development in contributing to the emotional well-being of the individual.

Loss and grief

As the previous sections have shown, domestic violence imposes emotional, physical, social and economic losses on those who experience it: loss of a sense of safety and security, trust in the world around them, personal identity and self-worth, perhaps of physical as well as emotional health, possessions, jobs, friends, family and community. Women saw these losses as having taken place gradually, almost imperceptibly, over the period of a relationship with someone for whom they had had, and often still had, feelings of love and who, at some time, had expressed similar feelings towards them. For those who take the difficult decision to leave the relationship for good, or who are forced to leave, whether they initially go to a refuge or not, there will be further significant and long-term emotional and material losses to face, which may play a crucial role in any decision-making process. This will include the relationship itself, where there may be feelings of shame and guilt, of love as well as fear and the loss of someone who has been the dominant figure in her life and played a major role in shaping her existence.

Leaving may also involve the loss of older children who are already living independently, or those who had to be left behind, of family, friends, any remaining support network, however small, pets, income from a job, or from their partner's employment. It is also likely to include the loss of a home which they had struggled hard to build up and keep together, often in the face of recurrent destruction of fabric and furniture by the abuser. The significance and impact of these multiple losses has been recognised by many other researchers in this field.[10]

For all the women who talked to me, there was the loss of a familiar environment – one which they knew and understood, however risky it had become. Many of them had travelled long distances to reach a refuge, either for reasons of safety, or to where there was accommodation available. For them this meant tearing up their roots and losing their own culture and way of life:

I cried all the way till when I got here… I knew I was crossing the county and I knew I wasn't going back there and it was… I don't know, I don't know how I felt, I just knew I were upset anyway. I were devastated because I was coming so far away from home and I wasn't going back and the kids weren't going back. (Val)

It can be difficult to comprehend the experience of loss on this scale. Women spoke of the need for time and space to take in all that had happened to them, to grieve for their losses and come to terms with their present situation. In listening to their stories, it became apparent to me that the pattern of recovery and rebuilding that they were going through mirrored, in its essentials, the pattern of loss, transition and recovery following bereavement. A number of versions of these progressions have been put forward,[11] but it can broadly be summarised as consisting of three fluid and interlinked phases:

1. An initial impact with feelings of intense shock, numbness, unreality and disbelief.

2. A transition period involving recognition of what has happened, a period of mourning, disorganisation and adjustment, with feelings of anger, loss, depression, lack of confidence and intense waves of emotional feeling, often unexpected and uncontrollable.

3. A time of reorganisation, recovery, implementing change and building a new way of life.

I have adopted the terms *Reception, Recognition* and *Reinvestment* to describe these three phases, as these seemed to me the words which best encapsulated the process occurring within and beyond the refuge setting for each woman. For some of them, a changed understanding of themselves and their role in society and a desire to develop their own abilities took place, during either the phase of *Recognition* or of *Reinvestment*. This could be identified in terms of Maslow's concept of self-actualisation (see Figure 1.1) and I have described this as *Realignment*.

In discussing the way an individual is likely to move through the phases of bereavement, Worden (1991) identified a number of tasks associated with the process, which both assist in coming to terms with the changed situation and require positive action on the part of the individual. The majority of these are emotional tasks: accepting what has happened; mourning the losses; adjusting to a new environment; and dealing with feelings about the person who has died. At the same time there are new and difficult practical issues that have to be faced: realising that the world has changed; taking on unfamiliar tasks and new roles; dealing with financial and social problems; and seeking a new identity and relationships. Just as in bereavement, these two strands (the emotional and the practical) run in parallel for women leaving an abusive relationship. There is a danger, however, that whereas in bereavement, as Stroebe and Schut (1999) point out, the difficulties and stresses of the practical problems may be overlooked, for women who experience domestic violence it is the practical aspects that become emphasised and the parallel and equal need for emotional support can be overlooked.

Research and practice in working with bereaved people[11] emphasises that these phases and tasks are not consecutive and boundaried. They represent a fluid and dynamic process of coping, which will be different in duration and support needs for each person within the context of their personal circumstances. The process will also be affected by any additional traumatic factors involved, as might be the case with murder, the death of a child, suicide, or accident. For women who have experienced domestic violence, it is the effects of abuse, discussed earlier, which make it more difficult to move forward – fears over personal safety, the availability of support and the loss of confidence, self-esteem and self-worth. Emotional support, therefore, needs to be directed at meeting these needs, in addition to understanding and working with the grief caused by the losses women have sustained and the practical tasks involved in moving on with their lives. As with bereavement, the rebuilding of their lives is not a speedy or straightforward process. As the next few chapters will show, women are likely to experience numerous periods when they return to their earlier feelings of sadness, confusion and self-doubt, as well as times when they are able to act with immense confidence and courage.

Loss, trauma and recovery

Unlike grieving after bereavement, which today is generally seen as a normal and socially acceptable process, domestic violence is still largely a taboo and stigmatised subject. Despite the efforts of campaigners over the past two decades and the positive approach of government, women are likely to be held back from disclosure by feelings of shame and guilt, particularly as they may be uncertain of the reaction they will get from family and friends, or from any agencies they may contact. Seeing the effects of domestic violence in terms of Maslow's ideas on human need can make it easier to understand why it can be difficult to reach out for support, or to decide to leave the relationship and why community support is of such importance.

For those who take the difficult decision to leave, there are major material and emotional problems to overcome. Placing these in the context of recovery from bereavement, made more traumatic and complex by the effects of domestic violence, can enable women to see their feelings as normal and understandable, given what they have been through, to locate themselves in a process with an ending and see that they are capable of acting to change things. The framework of understanding provided by these two perspectives can be utilised by agencies and organisations to understand why women may choose to return to, or remain in, the relationship, the emotional and the practical difficulties that have to be faced in staying or leaving and to provide effective and flexible support.

Summary

- Domestic violence can be physical, psychological, sexual, financial or emotional and these elements will often combine and reinforce each other. It normally follows a pattern of repeating and escalating incidents, whose unpredictability produces a state of constant fear and anxiety in those who experience it.

- The majority of incidents are perpetrated by men against women with whom they have, or have had, an intimate relationship. Violence and abuse may also occur within same-sex relationships, be carried out by women against male partners or former partners, or take place between members of the extended family.

- Although physical and sexual violence can cause permanent damage to health, women found that the mental impact of these acts and the emotional abuse of 'mind games', coercive control and manipulation were both harder to endure and more difficult to explain to others. Constant denigration and criticism had led to the loss of self-esteem, confidence and any sense of self-worth, while controlling and possessive behaviours had isolated them from family, friends and other potential sources of support.

- Women did not see themselves as powerless or passive within these situations. They took positive action to defuse tension and protect themselves and their children and utilised any opportunities that offered to maintain contact with others.

- Using Maslow's concept of human needs (Figure 1.1) offers a framework for understanding the effects of domestic violence and for effective support giving. It recognises the positive agency of the woman herself, her own capability to take action and her drive to improve the quality of her life, together with the importance of physical and mental safety and a supportive community.

- A diagnosis of post traumatic stress disorder (PTSD) can offer a way for women who need it to access specialist medical intervention, but may be inappropriate for the majority of women who experience domestic violence and may have adverse consequences in dealing with statutory bodies and other agencies.

- Women who leave an abusive relationship experience loss on material, emotional and personal levels. The process of recovery from these multiple losses is similar to that following bereavement, with fluid and overlapping phases spanning initial impact, transition and reintegration. In the context of domestic violence, I have identified these as *Reception, Recognition* and *Reinvestment.* Women may go on to develop a changed perception of themselves and their role in society, referred to here as *Realignment,* which can be seen as similar to Maslow's concept of self-actualisation.

- The process of recovery is made more complex and difficult by the way in which domestic violence has damaged confidence, self-esteem and feelings of self-worth. Support needs to work with these feelings as well as the difficulties created by the practical and emotional losses entailed in leaving the relationship.

- For women who experience domestic violence, whether they are in an abusive relationship or have left, support needs to be reliable and consistent, in order to rebuild confidence and trust and a sense that they are worthy of support. This support may need to be accessible on a long-term basis.

- Any support activity must prioritise physical and mental safety and work with the woman to rebuild her confidence and enable her to take control of her life. Emotional support is as important as practical assistance. Support should not be seen as limited to statutory and voluntary organisations, since individual and community support represent an important resource in recovery.

Notes

1. Stevens (1997); Yearnshaw (1997).
2. This definition is gender neutral, acknowledging the fact that men also suffer violence and abuse, both in same-sex relationships and from female intimates, as well as within the extended family. Statistical evidence, however, clearly shows that domestic violence is largely gender based and directed by men towards women (Dobash and Dobash 2000; Stanko 2000; Walby and Allen 2004). Findings from the 2001 British Crime Survey (Walby and Allen 2004) show that women form the vast majority of those suffering the heaviest abuse, multiple forms of abuse and repeat victimisation.
3. Dobash and Dobash (2000); Mirrlees-Black (1999); Walby and Allen (2004).
4. Humphreys and Thiara (2003); Kirkwood (1993); Mooney (2000).
5. Kirkwood (1993); Mooney (1993).
6. Other researchers (Dobash *et al.* 2000; Hoff 1990; Kirkwood 1993; Lempert 1996) have similarly noted positive coping strategies by women living in situations of domestic violence.
7. Lloyd (1995); Trevithick (2000).

8.　See Stark and Flitcraft (1996). Overviews of research into these links can be found in Golding (1999) and Cascardi, O'Leary and Schlee (1999) among others. PTSD, officially recognised as a diagnosis by the American Psychiatric Association in 1980, is associated with a cluster of symptoms, including suicidality, self-harm and depression, and also with anxiety states, panic attacks, fears over personal safety and a loss of confidence and self-esteem. It may additionally include a heightened state of vigilance, intrusive thoughts about the traumatic event or events, flashbacks and nightmares, overwhelming emotions alternating with numbness and a wide range of somatic symptoms (Dutton 1992; Herman 1992; Murphy 1997).

9.　In her analysis of PTSD and the path to recovery, Herman (1992) recognises the importance of community and peer support, together with movements for social justice and reform, but as Humphreys and Joseph (2004) point out, the significance of these broader based interventions appears to have been marginalised by professional and specialist groups seeking to retain control in this field. As Herman is at pains to point out, the vast majority of trauma sufferers do not receive professional help, but rebuild their lives using their individual strengths and resilience and the emotionally supportive relationships around them, including that of individuals with similar experiences and movements for social justice and reform.

10.　Charles (1994); Kelly (1988); Rai and Thiara (1997).

11.　Bowlby (1980); Murray Parkes (1986); Murray Parkes, Relf and Couldrick (1996); Shuchter and Zisook (1993).

Chapter 2

Starting the Journey

Making the decision to leave an abusive relationship is not a simple or easy choice. It involves considerations of risk and safety (is it more dangerous to stay or to go?), the availability of resources and support and a balance between losses and gains, made more difficult by the destructive effect that domestic violence has had on confidence and self-esteem. Some women may see leaving as a purely temporary measure, either to give themselves a brief respite before returning to the situation, or in the hope of shocking the abuser into a realisation of what is happening. Others may not have finally reached the conclusion that their relationship has ended and may well need to go through the process of leaving and returning to the relationship a number of times, in the hope of making it work, before they are ready to finally move on, assuming the hoped for changes in their partner's behaviour do not take place.[1] In all of these situations, the process of leaving may increase a woman's confidence in her ability to manage alone and provide time both to reflect on the relationship and to consider her own needs.

For 15 of the women who talked to me, this was their first visit to a refuge, although it was clear that a number of them had left the abusive situation previously, staying with friends or relatives and then returning to the relationship. Others had been in refuges before; six had made between two and three visits, one counted five visits and one woman thought she had been in at least seven. This group said that at each time of leaving they had regarded it as a final break, but had gone back for a variety of reasons, including the belief that the situation had changed or would change, and the financial and social difficulties which they saw as facing them. All of the women in the study were emphatic that their current decision to leave was final, but it is possible that one or more of them may have returned to the relationship at a later date.

Taking the decision

So why had they left now? Women commented that there had been a clear moment when they realised that they had to leave. For some of them, it had been the culmination of the leaving and returning process – a point at which they realised that things just couldn't go on in this way any longer:

> A lot of people don't have the family or friends to maybe use all the time, so maybe do go to a refuge and then go back and then go back again. But it does take, I think, one certain incident and one certain thing and when you just think…that's gone too far, or that's been too much or…you know, he's hurt me too much, or whatever it might be. And then you do realise, even though you have known, probably, for years, that it's never going to work. That you actually have to say well, no, that's it, I…whatever it might be, I can't take any more. (Jenny)

For others, like Stacey, it was the fear of imminent death that had given them the emotional strength to leave: 'The situation got so severe, I just thought my life was in extreme danger.' In other instances, the final driving force was anger. Janet decided 'enough was enough'. Amy was more specific: 'I thought, right, there's no way you're ever going to do this again.' For her, as for other women in their thirties, there was also a realisation that there must be more to life and that they were losing out on the chance of discovering their own potential. 'I actually walked away this time for myself. I just felt there was nothing in life for me, anymore, hardly.' Amalie agreed. 'I mean, I haven't had a life for the last 18 years. I've just had a beating, one long beating. And…now it's my turn. I mean, I want a life. And I'm sick to death of dancing to his tune.'

A small group of women had had the decision to leave taken out of their hands, either because their partner had (yet again) thrown them out and they had decided not to go back, or they had come to the refuge to ensure their own safety straight from hospital, or from court proceedings. Some of these women had now left the refuge and were living independently. The others felt that the action had helped them to make the break and they were unlikely to return.

Filling the information gap

One of the biggest obstacles to leaving was lack of information, mainly due to the isolation from any social contact which had been imposed on them by their abuser. This situation was made more difficult for those living in rural areas by restricted public transport services and lack of easy access to facilities such as doctors' surgeries or advice centres, where this information might have been available. The majority of those for whom this had been their first stay in a refuge had had no idea, to begin with, that refuges or support services which might help them existed:

> I had no idea that there were any women's refuges around, anywhere. I'd never seen one, never spoken to anyone who had been to one, didn't know what I was going to do when I had to leave home. I just spoke to my social worker, I said, I'm leaving, I don't know where I'm going. I could envisage myself sitting out on a bench somewhere...you know, not knowing what I was going to do. I had no money, nothing, in a terrible state of trauma. (Rachel)

Sometimes, as in Rachel's situation, the link was made by a social worker. Other sources of information had been the police, notices in GP surgeries, or clinics and, more unexpectedly, an assistant in a shoe shop who produced a phone book and looked up a helpline number. National and local helplines[2] had often been the first step towards seeking help and the support they had given to women in considering their options, making the decision to leave and finding a refuge, was remembered with appreciation:

> Knowing that there is actually somebody there to help you. It is hard to make that first call. It really is and...and I think the people who are on the phone, mostly, I think, are the most important people. Because, if you can't talk and feel trusted with them on the phone, you're not going to come to a refuge. And when I phoned the national line, they were brilliant. I could have broken down and cried and it was like...[*great sigh*]...somebody's actually listening to me. The helpline was great. Absolutely. (Liz)

The idea that someone had listened to them and believed what they said, without judging or criticising, had helped to boost confidence, name what was happening to them as domestic violence and recognise that it was not acceptable. Similar comments were made about advice centres. This 'giving permission', both to name the violence and that it was not inevitable, had been of immense importance to Stacey: 'I said to her, well, I just can't take any more. And she says, well, you don't have to. There's a place where you can go. That's where it all started.'

Women felt that had this information been more readily available to them, they might perhaps have taken action earlier. As Helga told me: 'I went through this for so many years, thinking I could either get beaten to death in a warm house, or freeze to death on the street, with nowhere else to go.' They were very clear that far more publicity and information needed to be made available,[3] although unsure as to how best this could be done. As Charmian said: 'Women are going through hell out there and they need to be told that there is somewhere they can get help.'

Making the break

> It's not as if…it isn't easy, you know. Anybody who thinks, oh well, all we've got to do is just, sort of, walk out the door and just get a train, or whatever, and just sort of toddle into a refuge, you know. And it just isn't like that; it isn't easy like that at all. Its one of the hardest things I've ever had to do. You know, because you just leave everything. (Barbara)

For all of the women, leaving had been an ordeal in itself, whether it was for the first time, or one of several such occasions. Some of them, having made the decision to leave, were given help by the police or, like Rachel, by a social worker. Three who had found their own way to a refuge had made a spur of the moment decision – 'just got up and run, that's what I did' said Charlene. Others had thought and planned meticulously, ringing the refuge until there was a vacancy, noting transport times, deciding who and what to tell and whether to involve other members of the family, working out what to say to their children and how to carry out their plans. One woman persuaded her husband to drive her and her suitcase to one of her older children for a 'short holiday', from where she contacted the refuge network. For others, there was a narrow 'window of opportunity' in which to bring all their planning together and make their escape, before their resolve failed:

> He went off to work and it was just one mad panic. I knew, if I didn't go that night, I wouldn't do it, I just wouldn't do it. And so, technically, yes, it was planned and I had support and back-up from me family. But if I hadn't, I'd never have gone. If I didn't…if I hadn't said, right, I'm going on that Sunday night, when he'd gone off to work, I wouldn't have done it. I couldn't get anything [together]. It was like, you thought this, oh, right. And that was going on all day. I've arranged to go on Sunday, so I'll just pack a few suitcases! Do you know? You can't do that! Because, if he'd found out, I wouldn't have been able to leave. So, when he went off to work on that Sunday morning, it was just a mad panic. QUICK! NOW! And we were putting things in bags and we just left. We just left. (Stacey)

Women arrived at their destinations emotionally and physically exhausted by the effort of leaving, with only what they could carry or put in a car, or, in many instances, with nothing at all.

Arriving at the refuge

The prevalent emotion on arriving, either for the first time or on a subsequent occasion, was fear, amounting in many cases to absolute terror. Some said they had felt physically sick. Not only was there the immediate fear that they might be found by their abuser and the possible consequences of that, but also the fear of the alien environment they were going to. Women were shocked by the fact that they had come to a refuge and uncertain as to whether they would be able to trust the other residents or, indeed, the workers. As Cathy, one of the refuge volunteers who had also experienced domestic violence, pointed out, having lived in an atmosphere of fear, isolation and uncertainty for so long such doubts were understandable:

> You don't know whether to trust these women or not. You don't know them, see, they're all strangers. And you don't know if they're trying to pull information out of you and on to Social, to tell them.

Additionally, there were concerns and fears around all they had lost and as to how they were going to manage with no food, no money and no belongings. For some, there were more long-term concerns about the future and the future of their children. This last was a particular concern for Asian women, where a child's marriage prospects might be seen to be affected by the woman's actions.[4] Coupled with fear was a general feeling of being so numbed, dazed and mentally confused by their experiences, that it was difficult to take anything in:

> You feel like you're absolutely shell-shocked. I just could not, for days and days, get my head round the fact that I was actually here. The whole thing is very strange and very weird and very, very surreal. Like being in a Ken Russell film or something, you know, floating through it. (Barbara)

> I think, looking back on it now, the first eight weeks, I just walked round in a daze. You know, I was doing things, getting the kids in school, but, it just didn't seem... I can't explain it, it was a horrible feeling. (Amy)

> My head was in bits and I didn't know whether I was coming or going. (Leanne)

These feelings of confusion and distress, similar to those which are generally experienced immediately after bereavement, have also been recognised in other research.[5]

Given the intensity of these feelings, the way in which the arrival at the refuge was managed was extremely important in helping women to settle down and feel comfortable, after the immense effort they had made to escape. Their immediate needs varied according to their situation. So, for Shelley, arriving with only the clothes she stood up in and having had to leave her children behind, the first need was for space and time to express her feelings. 'I couldn't stop crying or anything. They let me talk to them for hours, do you know what I mean? To get everything off your chest and that.' Where a move had been planned, even if executed in haste, it seemed easier to get straight into settling in:

> Katja [worker] met me and we went into the living room and she introduced herself and we sat talking and she took all me details and things and what had happened and explained things to me very thoroughly. What was expected and what I was expected to do and what they would do and stuff. And then she showed me to me room and stuff. (Stacey)

For all the new arrivals, the prime factors at this time were not feeling rushed, being listened to, believed and treated with respect as an individual who had been through a difficult and traumatic experience. Small welcoming gestures – a hug, being given a mug of tea – were vividly remembered months, even years, after they had occurred. 'Beautiful,' said Maryam. 'It was wicked.'

All the refuges maintained a limited stock of non-perishable food which could be made available to women and children to start them off and would loan small sums of money until other finance became available. At one refuge, the local branch of the Mother's Union provided a Welcome Box of toiletries and other essentials for any new arrivals, a small luxury which made a big difference. At another, the Welcome Pack for children included some new, age-appropriate toys which were theirs to keep.

Assessing support needs

Before the woman arrived at the refuge, a certain level of routine enquiry would generally have taken place, preferably with the woman herself, or with a referring agency such as the police, or social workers.[6] This would aim to broadly establish the details, circumstances and current situation of the family, the level of support which might be needed and whether that particular refuge was appropriate to meet their needs. The majority of refuges have an upper age limit on male children and it might also be difficult for some refuges to accommodate larger families. Considerations of suitability might, in some circumstances, include access. Although an increasing number of refuges are able to provide for women and children with mobility problems or physical impairments, many are still based in premises which cannot easily be modified. Women might also not be aware that there were refuges which catered specifically for their needs and might wish to consider this option. General refuges are, of course, open to all women, but the availability of specialist refuges offers women from particular minority communities, or special groups, a choice of which provision they would prefer to access.

Women from minority ethnic groups will not always choose to access specialist provision. Some may wish to do so while others may well prefer to access mainstream provision. Factors which may influence this decision include perceived racism in mainstream refuges, lack of trust in their own community, specific cultural or language needs and the approach which the woman takes towards integration.[7]

Discussing all these details in advance enabled workers to make a preliminary assessment of needs, to see if they had suitable accommodation and that they had the resources to provide appropriate support before offering a place. This would also require an assessment of the level of support currently required within the refuge; if additional support from external sources such as visits from health professionals or family aides could be made available and, in the case of communal refuges, the existing mix of residents. Dependencies relating to alcohol or drug use/misuse or mental health problems did not preclude acceptance (although using or supplying drugs on the premises was never tolerated), but very careful consideration had to be given to the woman's needs and the availability of staff resources, together with those from other agencies and the needs of the other residents.[8]

This preparatory work meant that any external support identified as necessary, such as family workers, Home Start volunteers or a visiting community psychiatric nurse, could begin to be put in place ready for when the family arrived at the refuge. In an emergency, it might not be possible to make these arrangements and any discussions would have to be carried out on arrival. All the groups involved in this research were committed to the Open Door policy of Women's Aid, in that no woman experiencing domestic violence would ever be turned away without some form of alternative provision. However, some workers were concerned that they had come to be regarded by other agencies and organisations as another part of general social provision and somewhere that women and children could be placed, without regard to what their problems were and if the refuge was the appropriate place for the family to be. Preliminary discussions, where the refuge was fully informed as to the range of support needed, enabled this to be checked to some extent. It was, however, acknowledged that more information and understanding would emerge after arrival at the refuge, which might result in a need to change the existing arrangements.

First steps

Workers were well aware of the importance of the initial period after arrival in easing the transition into the refuge and of establishing a relationship which would enable them to offer support in the future. Essential form filling (including licence or tenancy agreements), explanation of rules and conditions and any further discussion of her longer term needs had to be tailored to the immediate situation and level of distress, which might, as for Shelley, be extreme. Often these procedures were carried out in brief snatches, prioritising the most urgent and trying to ensure that the woman did not feel rushed or pressurised. Workers said that they would normally stay late, if necessary, to settle a woman in, a fact remembered with gratitude by several former and current residents. Workers were also on call to admit women after working hours, during the night and at weekends.

The first few weeks (or for some families a much longer period) after coming to the refuge were ones of immense need, during which a resident could be very demanding, both on an emotional and physical level and workers commented that during this period women needed to be able to access their support more frequently. This could be difficult where there was minimal or no weekend staffing. In fact, women who were admitted late on a Friday or over the weekend would sometimes have left by Monday before a longer period of face-to-face support was available. Women also commented on the way this group 'disappeared' and the sadness they felt when this happened. Offering the necessary emotional and practical support to new arrivals at this stage meant a period of intense and concentrated work. Where a number of families moved in within a short space of time, this could cause additional pressure on the workers and could have an impact on the amount of time available for other residents.

At the same time as dealing with all the emotional pressures of leaving the relationship and arriving at the refuge, women needed to cope with the physical and practical demands of the new situation – settling into the refuge, registering with the relevant agencies and completing forms for financial support (the dual sources of stress which have been similarly identified as occurring in bereavement). Many of them had never had the opportunity to deal with this type of paperwork before, or had never been allowed to, and they found it very difficult and confusing. Because of the circumstances of their arrival, they might well not have access to the information requested, or be able to provide the documents needed and, perhaps, be uncertain as to dates and places. Additionally, their experiences of domestic violence had resulted in a lack of confidence in their ability to state their needs and deal with the sort of questions that might be asked. Although support could be available from workers, women were encouraged to do these tasks for themselves, in order to build confidence and work towards an independent life. The response of the agency concerned could, therefore, have considerable immediate and long-term impact. A number of women reported that they had not received a sympathetic hearing. During one of my visits, a newly arrived resident had had to discuss her situation in a public area (as had happened to others) and was met with disbelief and a lack of understanding by a member of staff. This incident caused deep distress to the woman and anger and fear among the other residents, who were concerned that they might be treated in the same way.

Although there are many examples of good practice, service users have reported that agency responses can be patchy and inconsistent.[9] There is a real danger here that women may feel that they are being 'revictimised' by the agencies from whom they are seeking help and this may further reinforce their reluctance to seek assistance. Ensuring privacy and prioritising safety and confidentiality should be regarded as imperative for all agencies working with women who have experienced domestic violence.[10] Any breach of confidentiality, however inadvertent, can lead to the woman being traced, with potentially fatal consequences, or may force her to move on from a place where she had hoped to stay, as Amalie found. 'They [agency] sent a letter to my home address...and it had their address on it. Which was dead impressive. So he knew where I was. So I've got to move on...again.' Clearly, there are occasions where it might become necessary to break confidentiality (for example, in issues concerning child protection) or to share information with other agencies in the interests of the family. In such situations the woman should be fully aware of who is being informed and what information is being passed on and, if possible, she should be asked for her consent.

Safety

The overriding importance of safety was brought into sharp focus when women were asked what had been the single most significant factor about their arrival. There was complete unanimity that it was 'being safe'. They were in a place where their abuser could not gain entry and where violence of some sort was not a constant fear. Liz put it very simply: 'Being safe. The feeling of being safe. Not coming in and out of the door and having a fist or a bat waiting for you.' The refuge was also a place where they could feel emotionally as well as physically safe. Women were aware that their fragile mental state at this time meant they needed considerable emotional support as well as practical help when they arrived at the refuge. As Harriet explained: 'I was very emotionally bruised, let alone physically, and I felt that I'd arrived here and all the women that worked here just...just sort of picked me up and looked after me.' Women felt, without exception, that they had received this personal support, sometimes for the first time in their lives.

The physical and emotional support of other residents to women arriving at the refuge was also appreciated. This ranged from practical actions like cutting a pile of sandwiches, when they had been travelling all day with no food, to sitting with them over a cup of tea. It was observable, in the communal refuges, that residents were showing particular emotional and physical sensitivity to the needs of new arrivals. They were there to listen, or talk if this was appropriate, but would also understand if the new arrival needed space and to be left alone for a period of time. They were also sensitive to the fact that new arrivals needed extra help from workers:

> There's times when, you know, maybe a new lady coming in. And you know that she is more, maybe not more in need, but at that moment in time she needs them, and you can actually wait half an hour or an hour. (Jenny)

Perhaps the greatest gift to the new arrivals was the sharing of their experiences; the discovery that the newcomers were not, as they had believed, alone in what they had been going through:

> It was like a sigh of relief, when I came from that house and came here and knew there was other people in the same boat as me, that I could talk to. (Val)

> To know that I wasn't the only one and, you know, I wasn't…as daft and as stupid as he made out. Because we've all basically been through a similar type of thing. And together, talking to women in the similar type of situation, when you've made friends, you know you're not. (Stacey)

Reactions

Throughout the refuge stay, the emphasis from the workers was on providing a mentally and physically safe environment, believing women's accounts of their experiences without judging them and treating them as individuals worthy of respect. Women remembered clearly their initial reactions to this style of approach and the type of support they received – puzzled, a little surprised, but deeply appreciative:

> People treating you as though you're a worthy person, that's really been something I found very, very difficult to get my head around…that I am somebody that's worth being here, kind of thing. You get sort of emotional that…I suppose when people say they care about you, you know. And you think, God, I think they do and that's a shock and the fact that you're actually a worthy person and that your ideas and ideals matter and are important. And, you know, the respect. (Barbara)

Women linked this attitude of respect, so different from what they had been used to, with the way this had built up their own feelings of self-esteem and confidence, which had been eroded by the abuse they had experienced. Appreciation of the support they had been given on arrival was common to all of the women who spoke to me, even those who were highly critical of some other facets of refuge life. Both the practical and emotional support they had received were recalled in detailed and positive terms. In part, these recollections may have been coloured by the contrast with their previous existence and the dangers and difficulties they had gone through in order to escape. Women who might have felt differently may already have left, or preferred not to be interviewed. Nevertheless, the consistency and similarity of their accounts offers a basis for understanding the importance of this first phase of their journey and the approach which was most useful.

Once in the refuge, women felt safe and supported, without the need to plan for mortgage or rent payments and heating bills, or the overriding fear of physical or other forms of abuse. One reaction to this safety, from a very small number of women, was a period of 'going wild', as Cathy, a refuge volunteer, put it. The release from so much fear and concern had, in her view, led to a desire to test boundaries and rules, to see how far they could go and to enjoy to excess activities outside the refuge, such as clubbing and drinking, which had been prohibited by the abuser. It might also, she felt, be a way of avoiding working on emerging feelings of pain, awareness of the abuse and of how they had been manipulated in the past:

> She's going out drinking, thinking of men, having a laugh, going off clubbing, because, all of a sudden, she's been, she's able to do that, she's free, so she's gone absolutely wild. Wheee! I can understand that. But there is a time to stop and pull your socks up and think, right, well, I've had this time, I've done that. I'm going to start working now. Because it's not, you're not here for fun, yeah?

Similar behaviours were described by other workers and volunteers, who also commented that if such behaviour were carried to excess it affected other residents and could also endanger the security of the refuge. In talking with other women who had left abusive relationships, Kirkwood (1993) also found a small proportion who talked of a period of 'wildness' before they began to work on themselves. They too saw it as a chance to explore new freedoms and also as a way to cope with emerging feelings of pain and anger.

Similar 'testing' behaviour has been noted in children who have been experiencing or witnessing domestic violence (McGee 2000b). Although women who have experienced domestic violence will have had to cope with many restraints, some imposed by the abuser, some self-imposed in order to manage the situation, there will have been no containing boundaries to the experience of domestic violence because of the sheer unpredictability of what might happen and when. This period of 'going wild' may, therefore, also be used by some to re-establish and test their own boundaries as well as those of the refuge, before they can start making sense of their experiences, develop trust in those around them and start dealing with powerful emotions.

For the majority of women, this process of establishing boundaries for themselves and others was assisted by the welcome pack given to them on arrival and explained by the workers. This gave them written information about their rights and responsibilities, what was expected of them and what they could expect from the refuge workers and volunteers, as well as what they could do if they were not happy with any aspect of their stay or support. Although some of the restrictions could be irksome, they provided a clear framework. Women 'knew where they stood' and the guidelines were reinforced by workers who challenged inappropriate or inconsiderate behaviour. Maps and details of local transport, useful contact numbers and local information might also be supplied in order to help women situate themselves in their environment and understand the local structures.

Summary

- Staying, leaving, or returning to an abusive relationship presents complex issues around safety, the relationship itself and the emotional and practical problems to be faced. Woman may leave and return on a number of occasions before a final choice is made.

- Making the decision to leave may be driven by extremes of fear or anger, by the final realisation that the relationship is never going to work, or by the desire to build a life away from the violence.

- Lack of access to information was a major factor holding women back from leaving. Once located, helplines and advice centres were valued as a source of information and for the way in which they listened and responded to those who contacted them.

- Leaving the relationship, even when it had happened before, left women physically and mentally exhausted. They were fearful of being found, of those around them, the new environment and of the future. For varying periods of time afterwards, women felt numbed, confused and dazed, with no clear recollection of their actions. I have identified this phase, which I have termed *Reception*, as being similar to the initial reaction to bereavement.

- Refuge workers preferred to discuss their situation and needs with women before they arrived at the refuge. This enabled them to assess if suitable and appropriate accommodation was available and if there were specific support needs. Considerations might include mobility and access, the availability of specialist support and the needs of existing residents. The needs of women with mental health or drug or alcohol dependencies required careful assessment, but were not necessarily seen as a barrier to accessing the refuge.

- The refuge provided an environment which was both physically and mentally safe for women, where they could feel believed and heard and where they were treated with respect. This approach could be difficult to understand and accept, because it was so different from that which they had experienced in the past, but once it could be seen as genuine, this attitude built up the confidence and self-esteem which had been severely damaged by domestic violence.

- The period after arrival was one of intense and concentrated work, with both practical and emotional tasks to be dealt with. Where a number of admissions took place together, it could be difficult for workers to balance the needs of new arrivals against those of existing residents.

- Although the practical and emotional support given by other residents during this *Reception* phase was important, their greatest contribution was in helping newcomers to realise that others had had similar experiences and they were not, as they had believed, alone in what had been happening to them.

- A small number of women had explored their new freedom and tested their own boundaries and those of the refuge during a period of 'going wild'. This was also a way of postponing the need to deal with emerging feelings of pain and loss and testing boundaries.

- Agency responses needed a greater understanding of the practical and emotional effects of domestic violence and the problems that this might cause for service users in respect of missing or incomplete documentation and levels of personal confidence.

- Issues around privacy, safety and confidentiality were particularly important, since inadvertent disclosure could lead to serious consequences if the woman were traced. If there was a need to share information with other agencies, the woman needed to be fully informed as to what was being divulged and to whom, and her consent obtained if possible.

Notes

1. Similar findings have been obtained by other researchers (Batsleer *et al.* 2002; Dobash and Dobash 1979; Kirkwood 1993).

2. Since these interviews took place, a freephone 24-hour National Domestic Violence Helpline (0808 2000 247) has been established, run in partnership between Women's Aid and Refuge. Other local and national helplines are available and details of some of these can be found in Appendix 3, together with other resource materials.

3. Similar views have been expressed by the residents and ex-residents in other refuges and by users of outreach services (Humphreys and Thiara 2002; Lodge, Goodwin and Pearson 2001; McGee 2000a; Rai and Thiara 1997). Many groups, inter-agency fora and health projects, amongst others, are pioneering imaginative ways of enabling women to access this information. This has included using sites such as the backs of bus tickets, bus stickers, rent books, posters in various women-only facilities and the development of tiny contact cards which can be easily concealed. Although there is clearly an urgent need for such information to be made more widely available, it needs to

be recognised that this has considerable resource implications since media publicity (storylines or other information) has been shown to result in increased calls to helplines.

4. That this fear is common among many Asian women fleeing domestic violence has been confirmed in consultative workshops by specialist Asian refuges and by the research carried out by Batsleer *et al.* (2002).

5. Binney, Harkell and Nixon (1981); Pahl (1978). In their more detailed examination of the process of arrival, Rai and Thiara (1997) additionally comment on the feelings of unreality and detachment experienced by new arrivals.

6. Women's Aid refuges prefer to deal directly with the woman herself. Other organisations which provide safe accommodation feel that referral via social services or other statutory or professional agencies offers additional screening of potential residents.

7. Batsleer *et al.* (2002); Rai and Thiara (1997).

8. As Barron (2004) has pointed out, women who experience domestic violence and also have mental health problems and/or alcohol and/or drug dependencies have complex support needs. Although some refuges can meet these needs and have specially trained support staff, many provide shared facilities that may not always be suitable for the needs of this group. The staff may not be able to offer the higher degree of support that may be required by these women. A specially designed refuge, run by The Haven, Wolverhampton, opened in 2005 to provide a specialist, integrated support system for women with mild/short-term mental health problems caused by domestic abuse and to cater for the needs of their children.

9. Bossy and Coleman (2000); Humphreys and Thiara (2002).

10. In her study of housing and domestic violence Davis (2003) has drawn attention to this element in the work of housing associations, but it can be seen as equally relevant to the work of other agencies.

Chapter 3

Exploring the Route

As the initial impact of leaving the relationship and arriving at the refuge lessened, women moved gradually into a phase which I have termed *Recognition*; to a point where they became more able to take stock of themselves and their situation, the resources that were available to them, and to think about what they wanted to do next. At the same time as dealing with these practical considerations, however, they had to cope with the destructive effect the abuse had had on their confidence and self-esteem and the additional emotional distress caused by leaving the relationship. Feelings of loss and anger, which had been submerged by shock and numbness on arrival in the refuge, became more apparent. Women also found that their moods could swing between confident highs and deep, depressive, lows without apparent warning in a way that was extremely frightening. These feelings formed a constant background to refuge life and impacted on every other aspect of the women's lives. In particular, they influenced the nature of the support that was needed, and whether a woman was able to make use of the resources that were on offer.

Loss

In making the decision to leave, women had already thought about some of the losses they would face, but it was only now that the full extent of all which had gone began to be recognised. Women mourned the loss of their homes in a way that showed just how much these had meant to them and the efforts that had gone into each one. In some ways, as Jenny commented, it was the loss of their small personal possessions and mementos that hurt most:

> Even if it's not the best house in the world, it's just everything you've wanted, everything you've worked for, all you've got together. No matter how you got your house, or what you have in your house, it's your own. And it could be just a sofa and a bed, but it's your home. And no matter how much or how little you've got…because we didn't have a great deal

because he was always spending the money on other things, but even if you just have a small little house with a few little bits that are really important, it's what you've made it. And having to leave personal belongings; not so much furniture, but I remember, when my little boy was about a year, he did a little drawing and stuff and we had it, actually, up on the wall in a little frame. I'd love to have that, but it's gone. It's just all gone.

Many items of this nature were irreplaceable, but they were well aware that making good even some of their material losses would be an uphill struggle. Those who had been in paid employment had left their work to come to the refuge and money from a partner's job, or joint social income, were no longer accessible. They would need, initially, to rely on benefit payments and faced the prospect of years of managing on a low income. Since most of them had been able to bring very little with them, any money they received had to stretch to replacing essential possessions and additional clothing for themselves and their children, as well as feeding the family, before perhaps beginning to save towards items for a new home.

Only two of the women had been able to come to a refuge near their homes and hoped to return, with legal protection, or be rehoused in a nearby location, but away from their abuser. The rest had travelled away from their local area; almost half of them had travelled more than 100 miles to reach the refuge they were in. City and country both seemed alien environments to those who had not experienced them before, and with the loss of their familiar setting they had also left familiar faces, children who had had to be left behind, pets and any casual contacts. As Liz explained: 'I've come a long way, away from everything I know. I don't know a soul. And it's tough.' For some women, the fear and anxiety caused by domestic violence had driven them to take this severing of ties further. In order to escape as finally as possible from their abusers, they had completely changed their names and identities. In one way this marked the start of a new life for them, but it also meant that they had had to 'bury' their previous selves before taking on the new identity. Other women hoped that they might, eventually, be able to re-establish contact with family and friends. These women now have to face a lifetime of concealment, secrecy and probably continued isolation from those they had known in their previous existence.

For all the women, there was the pain and distress of having left a relationship in which they had invested so much emotional capital and where, for many of them, feelings of love and concern still existed. They had also to come to terms with the way in which violence and abuse had eroded their sense of self, their individuality and personal integrity. As their accounts in Chapter 1 showed, women recognised that their experiences of abuse had led to a total loss of self-confidence, self-respect and self-esteem. Barbara, who had left after many years of emotional abuse, was clear about what had happened: 'You have so many years of being told you're rubbish. And you believe it.' As a result, when they arrived at the refuge, women felt that they had been drained of everything. Commenting on this emptiness, several of them said: 'You feel you're nothing when you come here.' Regaining this sense of self-worth and the confidence to act and make independent choices, from such a low point, was a slow and difficult process for women as one volunteer worker, Helen, recognised: 'Sometimes it takes an awfully long time for them to get it out of their head that they are worthless. And we've got to build them up.'

As the impact of all these losses – material, emotional and personal – became clearer, women talked of needing a period of time to mourn over all that they had lost. For some, this grief was expressed in talking to other women, to workers, counsellors and volunteers. Several had started to keep journals where they were able to record their feelings and at least one had found an outlet in writing poetry for her private use. Writing down how they felt and their gradually changing perceptions, they told me, had been very powerful and had the added advantage that they could look back and see the advances they were making. It was also helpful, when they were feeling depressed and lonely, to see that they had successfully come through similar patches before.

Anger

Anger is a part of the natural process of grief and women, understandably, felt very angry over what had happened to them and the physical and emotional situation they now found themselves in. It seemed to them that, with the loss of their homes and lifestyle, together with their identity and support systems, they were the ones being punished, rather than the abusers:

> Obviously you have to keep the doors locked, you've got bars at the windows. We used to…we'd say, after all we'd been through, you wouldn't have got so long if you done 'em in, through self-preservation, a spur of the moment. You'd get a few months in prison, let out, and you'd have had all the wonderful treatment that they get in prison, university degree and all sorts you could get. Sports facilities…and here we are dumped in this place with bars at the windows and locked doors. (Rachel)

Only three of the women displayed high and open levels of anger and aggressive behaviour during the interviews. For one, this was related to tensions with other residents, including 'missing' food from the communal freezer. Another had been in the refuge for some months and was angry with the local council for not rehousing her more quickly. The third had had a specific problem, discussed later in this chapter, where she felt that she had not received enough support from workers. Some of these difficulties may have been part of the emotional 'ebb and flow' within the women themselves, or of stresses and tensions within the refuge. Interviews at a different time might have revealed a different picture, with more or less anger being expressed openly. It is also possible that women who displayed similar levels of hostility may already have been asked to leave because of inappropriate behaviour, found themselves unable to live in the refuge environment and left, or preferred not to be interviewed.

Anger at some aspect of their past or current experience was, however, mentioned in all of the interviews and was expressed by residents and ex-residents towards various individuals and objects, including their abusers and the systems and agencies that were seen as having failed them and, in some aspects, were continuing to do so. The strong views expressed by some residents about any perceived lack of support and restricted access to workers may also be a reflection of these deep feelings of anger. Instances of self-harming, ranging from mild to severe, which were noticeable in the refuges, can also be seen as indicating repressed feelings of anger and frustration.[1]

Many women do block legitimate angry feelings during their experience of domestic violence, feeling that expressing their anger while in the abusive situation may well make things worse. Research has suggested that this anger may come out slowly and in indirect ways when it feels safer to express it.[2] Among the counsellors who were working with residents and ex-residents, there was a recognition that women needed to be able to express their feelings of anger in a safe environment and that it was important for them to learn effective and proactive ways to handle conflict in everyday life, so that they were less vulnerable to exploitation and abuse once they had left the refuge.

Oscillating emotions

All the women talked of the way in which their emotions were confused, erratic and unstable, even when they had been in the refuge for a considerable time. Although the move had given them much needed physical safety, they felt that their emotional and mental safety and stability were still very precarious. An apparently trivial incident could occur and it was not possible for them to predict if they would be able to handle it rationally, or alternatively be deeply upset. Feelings changed from day to day and within each day, sometimes from hour to hour. This emotional 'roller-coaster' was naturally hard for them to understand and frightening, not only because of its unpredictability, but also because they wondered if all the 'emotional baggage' would ever go away, or if they had some type of mental problem:

> It can be something and nothing. You might burn your tea or something and that could be it. You just feel, oh, God, you know. It can be the smallest things, really…sets you onto feeling very down and a bit, a bit glum. (Jenny)

And it's wondering whether that will ever go because…I mean sometimes, some days I get up and I'm, I'll get up and I am in a good mood and I'm fine and then other days I'll get up and it'll be like I won't be, I'll start crying all day and I'll be thinking, well, why did you do it and, you know… I'm like, so mixed up in my mind and sometimes I think, ah, it's really unfair, I'd just like to go and tell him, you know, like everything's not alright because me head's totally…mashed. (Val)

Unpredictable and intense mood swings are recognised as forming part of grieving a loss and as continuing over an extended period. This was certainly the case for the women who had left the refuge, who talked of the difficulties that these changes could still create for them.

During the weeks I spent in each refuge, I became very aware of this oscillation, of the way in which emotions could radically change from high to low, or vice versa, over a very short period of time and the effect this would have on women's appearance, behaviour and relationships within the refuge. Workers saw this pattern repeated constantly and found it stressful and draining to see a woman who was starting to build up her confidence, suddenly crash down over something comparatively small, but perceived by her to be an immense problem. In addition, it could also make it difficult for them to assess the appropriate level of practical and emotional support which a woman needed at any given time.

Safety, trust and empowerment[3]

Before women could move forward into discussing options and plans for the future, they needed to feel mentally secure and comfortable with the refuge workers and begin to trust them. This process required time and space for reflection and could take weeks or even months, depending on each woman. For Liz, it was a long struggle: 'Basically, I just didn't trust *anybody*. I wanted to be safe and I wasn't letting anybody spoil it for me. It's taken all of five months!' Physical safety remained of prime importance to all the women. They were still nervous of being traced and of possible retribution,[4] but inside the building the way they were treated enabled them to feel more emotionally secure and relaxed:

Feeling free and safer and able to do what I want when I wanted. I think the best thing, really, if you put it down to just basic things, it's waking up in the morning without that person laid next to you, waking you up…and knowing, really, that the day is just going to get worse and worse and worse and worse… Just knowing, really, that you can wake up without all that. Just waking up alone. (Jenny)

As a crucial part of the way they approached their work and built these feelings of trust and safety, workers identified the use of counselling skills – active listening, empathy and a non-judgemental attitude – to create a supportive environment where this development could take place. These skills were employed in the way information and encouragement were offered, options debated and strategies for moving on, mentally and physically, discussed. This style of support was seen as closely related to, but different from, the formal counselling available for women, and workers drew a clear distinction between the two activities.[5]

With the development of trust during this time, and mental safety reinforcing physical security, women felt their perceptions of the refuge staff changed and that they could bring out and discuss events, people and situations which may have been distorted or concealed on arrival. Residents valued the knowledge and expertise of workers, but also the fact that they were never pushed into taking a course of action but could discuss their ideas freely:

> They're not there saying you've got to do this and you've got do that. They're just there. You go to them and say well, I want do this, what you think? Because they've had, like, experience there, so...yes. And I think that's what women need. They don't need someone dictating what they should and shouldn't do, when they come into a refuge. (Eve)

Being treated with respect and as responsible members of society was seen by workers as the key to empowering women and giving them the confidence to make their own choices. 'Respect' was not, however, just about attitude and approach. The women were emphatic that it included refuge workers being honest and 'upfront' about what was happening to any applications, possible consequences of any decisions or actions that they might be considering and clear explanations of where the refuge stood in any situation (for example, in regard to child protection), however difficult and perhaps unpleasant it might be to have to hear this. They felt they knew where they stood, that firm boundaries had been established and what they could expect from the workers. This was contrasted with the behaviour of other agencies that were often seen as failing to keep them informed or, in their view, talking to other people about them without informing them, or asking for their consent. Leanne was glad to know where she stood: 'Other people sort of, go behind your backs, but they've always been upfront with me, told me exactly what they think, laid the ground rules down.'

Praise and encouragement, together with emotional support, formed a complete contrast to the destructive interrogation and criticism which women had experienced in the past, enabling them to build self-esteem and gradually become more able to take decisions and action for themselves. This was not, however, an easy option for women who had frequently not been permitted to act for themselves, even to the extent of using the telephone. Maggie's plaintive comment, echoed by many women was: 'No one will tell me what to do.' Workers such as Janna, however, saw this as part of the process of learning to make choices and empowerment: 'They're always asking us for the answers and it's something we can't give them.' In retrospect, the majority of women could see that being encouraged to do things for themselves, and make their own decisions, had been the best way of gaining confidence in their own abilities to take control of their lives and live independently on leaving the refuge. Most were essentially realistic about the fact that, whatever degree of support on a practical or emotional, level they received, there were things that they had to come to terms with on their own:

> But, yes, I mean things, you do, you find that when you do come here, things…it *is* tough. I mean, however much support you get, you know, you've got to live with yourself, you've got to try and fathom things out in your head and it's…none of it is easy. (Barbara)

Changing needs

After the initial reception period was over, practical tasks took on a different focus. Together with workers, women would develop an individual support plan (ISP) setting out their aims, the steps to take in order to achieve these in the short, medium and long term and the degree of support they felt would be necessary during this process. Women needed to establish a routine for their children, arrange, if necessary, for nursery or school places and register with health professionals. Legal issues such as injunctions or divorce proceedings might need to be considered or criminal charges might be pending. There was also the future to think about – perhaps arranging for the temporary storage of property, deciding the best options for where to live and making applications for housing. In all these situations, women found that they had to learn, or relearn, the skills necessary for independent living such as form filling, making applications, negotiating, contacting organisations and services, financial management and so on. These were skills they had frequently not been allowed to exercise by their abuser. Workers defined their role during this period as providing both emotional support and practical information, building confidence and encouraging women to handle their own problems with support and advice. They saw themselves as assisting women to move along a continuum from the sense of being and having nothing, which was so evident upon arrival, to a degree of confidence that they could leave the refuge and live independently. The conflicting pressures of practical problems and the changing emotional stresses discussed earlier, however, meant that this was never likely to be a straight line progression, but a dynamic process. Women moved forward and back, as they themselves commented, sometimes going back to their feelings on arrival at the refuge and at others moving purposefully towards a goal:

> Sometimes I feel like on a high, where I just do everything and I do it by myself with no one's help. And sometimes I feel just on a low, where it's like…come on…you need that greater…push. (Maryam)

One of the workers, Frances, suggested the process was 'like looping the loop, the emphasis is onward and upward, but you will have downward loops as well, on your way up'.

Again, counselling skills were seen as important in the way support was delivered, how women were assisted to gather information and make choices and to implement their own strategies for change, without feeling that they were being told what to do. Workers needed immense skill to be able to balance between support leading towards independence and that which might encourage continuing dependency; knowing when to gently challenge a woman to use her personal strengths and when a higher degree of support or even advocacy was needed. This complex situation is made more difficult by the fact that every woman who comes to the refuge will have different support needs and her individual needs will also vary from day to day, depending on her problems and her emotional reactions to them.

Workers in all the refuges felt that the key factor in working in this situation was to place the woman's needs and her perceptions of her problems at the centre of their work and to refrain from imposing solutions that might appear obvious to them, but which might not feel appropriate, for whatever reason, to the woman concerned. They needed to be open and aware of the needs of each woman and flexible enough to respond appropriately. Nevertheless, in the often relentless pressure of daily refuge life, it was not always easy to get the balance right. Women who on the surface seemed in control might be feeling in need of additional support; yet an unwanted approach might be seen as an intrusion into privacy and disempowering in its effect. To assess and deal with this situation was seen as more difficult in refuges with self-contained accommodation, if a woman chose not to come into the office or make contact with workers or volunteers in some other way. Inevitably, a few women felt that their ability to handle their problems had been overestimated:

> Okay, I appreciate the fact that they said…okay, it's good that you learn like to be…to deal with your own matters, because once…you don't get that type of support like they offer here. You'll be all on your own then. Okay, I accept this but…maybe it's an easy alternative for them. You know, you look all right, you look like you're all right and you're really a strong person. But inside of yourself, you might not be. You know? (Hayley)

On the other hand, workers were of the opinion that some women expected everything to be done for them:

That's a fine line, because some women will tell you that they want you to do this, this and this, but they don't need you to do this, this and this and it's about making out if that woman is…it's very subjective. (Jay, worker)

Attempting to reach and maintain a balance between all these factors could be difficult and frustrating for workers, particularly in view of the other pressures on their time and the overall stress of working in the refuge environment. They needed to feel supported within their work team and that their work was valued by the rest of the organisation if they were to be able to continue to offer this type of help.

Advocacy[6]

As the incidents recounted in Chapter 2 show, a poor response from statutory and other agencies to women experiencing domestic violence will affect not only the woman who experiences it, but also have a 'knock-on' effect on the other residents. Although workers aimed to support and empower women to take action for themselves when dealing with these agencies (as they would have to do in the future), they accepted that there were times when it was necessary for them to go beyond this and work as advocates with, and on behalf of, women to help them obtain a just solution to problems, or their rightful entitlements. Given the emotional and practical difficulties that residents already had to surmount, the extra resources of strength and energy needed were sometimes just not available to them. As Kelly and Humphreys point out: 'Negotiating with powerful organisations can be anything but empowering' (2001, p.246).

Workers commented that successful interventions required knowledge, persistence and a determination not to be 'fobbed off'. They recognised their frequent successes as a tribute to their professionalism, but they were aware that in providing this support, even when working as partners with the woman, there was the potential to undermine her confidence and ability to act for herself. Areas where advocacy was particularly valued by women included occasions when residents felt they were being passed from one agency to another without any actual attempt to help them, and in representing their views to agencies who insisted on using terms and jargon which they did not understand. Workers were also seen as being influential in cases where a number of agencies were involved:

The social workers and people like that weren't doing what they were supposed to. Weren't giving me…telling me the dates of the meetings, the dates of this, that and the other and keeping me in the dark about a lot of things and then Janna and Oriel got on the phone and Kim [workers] and that was it…the bits all started to come into a picture. You know, they really went to work on it. (Shelley)

Advocacy and support in legal and court proceedings was also valued by the very small number of women involved in divorce or custody hearings, but it was interesting to note that support in taking legal action was not the first thing that came to mind when women were asked about support needs or difficulties. This may be due to a reluctance to take legal action or a doubt as to its efficacy, or perhaps to the greater importance to them of getting on with their own lives.

Where advocacy was necessary, it was seen by workers as only one part of the overall aim of empowering women to take control of their own lives and feel confident in acting as their own advocates. Practical and emotional support and advocacy, delivered using counselling skills, can be seen as working together to achieve this. Leanne, whose young son had acute behavioural problems at school and in the refuge, explained how it had worked for her, once she felt able to trust and work with one of the refuge staff:

> Alma [worker] and me, we've got like a good strategy plan what they can all do to help me. Because he was walking out of school when he was upset. Alma said like it's just a matter of praising him and building his confidence. I'll sit and do work with him, reading and writing. But, yeah, it's like I aren't too good at talking to teachers and stuff, so Alma come with me and she could put it in my terms and when they were using all the big posh words, she could say, well, basically, they're saying this… I'm a lot more confident than I was about it. (Leanne)

It was apparent, however, that at times, the balance between all these factors could go badly wrong, as in the situation faced by Hayley, one of the three women whose open anger was mentioned earlier and who had previously commented on what she had felt was an unacknowledged need for support:

> I was trying to tell them, Look, this is happening, but nobody, really like, was interested. And I thought, oh my God, how'm I gonna do that and I knew it was bad enough, because the court order was there and the neighbourhood office was saying, look, there's gonna be a court hearing. So I started saying, no, this is not good, this is not… It hasn't helped. We just about got it together. And the bailiff was just gonna come into my house and take all my stuff away. So we just got in before, with a solicitor. (Hayley)

The situation was rescued at the last minute, when workers realised what was happening, but the incident has left Hayley feeling angry, frustrated and disempowered.

Mutual support

When women first came to the refuge, the physical and emotional support they received from other women was extremely important to them, particularly in showing them that they were not alone in what they had gone through and that they were not mad or stupid as they had repeatedly been told. As women began to recover from the initial impact of arrival in the refuge, support between them and the other residents became more reciprocal and they were able in their turn to offer reassurance and support to new arrivals. It was clearly important to their evolving self-esteem to feel they had something of worth to offer to others and that their contribution was welcomed.

For women who had been in the refuge for some time, mutual support became a very important part of their lives. Physical company (watching television, going shopping together) provided an antidote to the isolation that many of them had been subjected to. The knowledge that another resident would be there for them at bad times was a source of emotional strength. Two of the women specifically commented on the strength and inspiration they had drawn from meeting women in their sixties and seventies who had found the courage to leave their relationships after many years of physical and emotional abuse. Three other residents told me that had it not been for the support of the other women and the solid reasons they gave for remaining in the refuge, they would at some stage during their stay have gone back to their abuser because of the stresses caused by the practical and emotional problems they encountered and the fear of an uncertain future:

> I got all packed, I was all packed and I was going to go. And I thought, ooh, you know, it was just...stuff was getting on top of me and I, and it just seemed that, you know, I felt my future, you know, and I really didn't like the look of it. And I suppose it kind of seemed easier, but anyway we had sort of like a little meeting down here and I was persuaded to stay. No, I mean, they gave me good reasons to stay and I said I would actually think about it. Seriously give those pointers that they...give that serious consideration and I did and I thought, yeah, you're right on that one. But it wasn't just, oh, please stay, we all love you, wasn't anything like...well, they did say that, but, I mean it was good solid reasons. (Barbara)

Mutual support of this kind has been a key element in the work of Women's Aid refuges throughout their history and research has consistently commented on the strength that women have drawn from each other and from their shared experience.[7] Nevertheless, residents were also honest and realistic about the difficulties that could arise with mutual support when there was tension or conflict resulting from the living arrangements within the refuge. They pointed out that the value of mutual support very much depended on the mix of women in the refuge at any one time. As Leanne commented: 'I mean, you're not guaranteed to get on with everybody, but you don't anyway, do you?'

Despite the problems and difficulties that could arise, residents and ex-residents alike saw mutual support and strength as well as the companionship gained from other women as being one of the most important factors in helping them to recover from their experiences and move forward with their lives, complementing the practical and emotional support, information and advocacy provided by the refuge workers and volunteers. The sole exception to this view was one of the women whose open anger was mentioned earlier who had experienced problems over 'missing' food. She was emphatic:

> I don't mix with no one, really. I might see them and say, hello, or, are you going down the shop or, are you going to the bus stop, but I say I don't owe it to the women in here… I keep myself to myself… I'm not that partial to them, to tell the truth. (Maryam)

It may be that her views had been shaped by her experiences within the refuge or outside, but this attitude was not shared by the other two residents who were openly angry, or by any other of the women who talked to me.

One interesting addition to the way women supported each other, which I saw developing over the 18-month period of the field research, was the growth in the use of texting on mobile telephones. This took place between women in the refuge and ex-residents and from residents who were outside the refuge on business texting residents or workers for support and advice. It was not limited to the younger residents and was apparently becoming a common and accepted way of keeping in touch and obtaining support. This creation of a 'mobile' (in both senses) support system that 'goes with' a woman may, perhaps, indicate the development of a different aspect of mutual support, with the concept of a network of residents, ex-residents and workers.

Summary

- As the initial impact of leaving the relationship and arriving at the refuge lessened, women moved into a phase of *Recognition*; a point where they became more able to take stock of themselves and their situation, the resources they had, or could access and to think about what they wanted to do next.

- At the same time as these practical considerations, however, they had to cope both with the destructive effect which the abuse had had on their confidence and self-esteem and the additional emotional distress caused by leaving the relationship. Rebuilding a sense of confidence and self-worth was a long-term process which was crucial in helping women to take control of their lives and live independently.

- Feelings of material, emotional and personal loss, which had been submerged by shock and numbness on arrival in the refuge, became more apparent and needed to be mourned.

- Previously suppressed anger was directed at a range of individuals and organisations and unpredictable and uncontrollable emotional surges could change emotions from high to low from hour to hour. This had an impact on day-to-day reactions to events and the ability to handle challenges.

- Although physical security was the first priority, a sense of mental safety was also important. In order to discuss their situation and their options fully, women needed to feel confident that they could trust those around them to be consistent, predictable and reliable.

- Women valued an approach from workers and agencies which treated them with respect and as responsible, autonomous members of society. Respect included open and honest communication, clarity of information and being kept fully informed of what was happening. They considered emotional support to be as important as practical assistance in empowering them to move forward.

- Moving forward was not a linear progression, but a fluid and dynamic process where women might return to feelings of self-doubt and shock before making further progress.

- Workers aimed to support women to define their own needs and make independent choices. This was not easy for those who had not previously been allowed to act for themselves. Each woman had different support needs depending on her personal circumstances and these needs were also different for each woman at different times, requiring constant reassessment of the level and type of support needed.

- Lack of knowledge and confidence meant that advocacy by workers was sometimes needed, in addition to practical and emotional support, but the aim was always to encourage women to act independently and gain confidence in handling situations for themselves.

- The support and understanding of other women who had experienced domestic violence was a valued source of strength and inspiration, both emotionally and on a practical level. A further and increasing source of support was coming from the use of mobile phones.

Notes

1. Arnold and Magill (2000); Heath (2003).

2. Kirkwood (1993); Walker (1993).

3. Empowerment has come to be interpreted in a number of ways, depending on the context and setting in which it is used and there is a considerable body of literature on the subject. In this case, it refers to the process of working in partnership with women to help them to access resources and information and supporting them in acquiring the necessary skills and confidence to take their own decisions and to handle the situations they would meet on leaving the refuge.

4. It was possible that where the abuser knew or obtained their mobile phone number, threats could still reach women inside the refuge. In one group it had become customary for women to exchange phones with other residents to counter this threat to their mental safety and other refuges have supplied new SIM cards. Mobile phones or other tracking devices can also be used to trace women, a point discussed further in Chapter 7.

5. Counselling skills and other supportive relationships such as befriending, the provision of advice and guidance, advocacy and coaching differ from the formal counselling discussed in Chapter 4. These skills are normally applied in a much more informal process, using the communication and relationship skills which derive from and are used in counselling and applying them to enhance the performance of another role, such as tutor, nurse, teacher, refuge worker or friend (Bond 2000; Feltham 2000).

6. Advocacy, like empowerment, is a word capable of multiple interpretations, dependent on context. Advocacy, as the term is used here, accepts that a woman has needs and entitlements from a variety of organisations, agencies and statutory bodies. She may not, for a variety of reasons, have the knowledge, expertise or confidence to fight for her rights, or to receive a fair hearing. In this situation, advocacy goes beyond empowerment and works with the woman to remedy this and provide additional impetus.

7. Binney *et al.* (1981); Bossy and Coleman (2000); Charles (1994); Clifton (1985); Malos and Hague (1993).

Chapter 4

Someone to Talk to, Someone to Listen

Isolation from any social contact had formed a major part of the abuse that women had experienced. Everyday activities – using the telephone, talking to people they met on the street, visiting friends or family – were either forbidden, or made extremely difficult, perhaps by restricting the available spending money, or by constant surveillance and interrogation. Visitors to the home were implicitly or actively discouraged. As a result women were cut off from most normal sources of conversation, including any contact which might have offered an independent perspective on what was happening, or provided information and support. They became increasingly dependent on their abuser for communication, which was usually negative in nature and destructive of their confidence and self-esteem. Once at the refuge, they were actively seeking to end this isolation, to make verbal and emotional contact with other people and to restore their links to society. This drive to reach out to others was identified by Maslow (1987) as one of the basic needs of human beings; the desire not just to survive, but to seek to make connections to others and to belong to a community (Figure 1.1, p.22).

Contact with others seemed to be needed on three levels. First, normal, everyday conversation, then supportive talk – dealing with what had happened and planning for the future and finally, what might be described as healing talk – a space where they could reflect on their experiences and learn to deal with their feelings in their own way. For those women who had children with them, it was also important to work on the communication between them, so that they could connect as a family. Women distinguished between these different types of talk and saw all of them as being needed in helping them to rebuild their lives. The levels of contact were not clearly separated. A conversation with a worker might move from casual to supportive and back again. Moments of insight and personal growth might occur in late-night talks with other residents, as well as in formal or informal counselling sessions. Recognising that they needed these different levels of dialogue, women created networks of communication and support from a variety of sources, both within and beyond the refuge.

Mutual support

As previous chapters have shown, the support of other residents, both on arrival and throughout their stay in the refuge, was highly valued. It showed women that they were not alone in what they had endured and provided strength and support within the refuge, companionship and a chance to resume the sort of everyday conversation which might be expected in daily life – the weather, health, shopping and television, as well as what was happening in the refuge. In all the communal refuges, talking together late into the night, as well as at other times, was a recurring theme, turning to advantage the feelings of restlessness and inability to sleep which were common among all the women.[1] Discussions included what had happened to them and their experiences of abuse, enabling them to 'talk it out' and gain a new perspective, but there was also time to talk about the future and to exchange ideas, gain information and learn from what others had done. Some of this information was being passed down through several intakes of refuge residents, and a body of 'refuge lore' seemed to be developing. General social and political discussion also took place about what was going on in the world outside the refuge – 'setting the world to rights', as several of them put it. During this time, a strong bond developed between many of the women:

> You do build up a very strong relationship with other people, if you…you know, with some others…you sort of gel with somebody, you kind of make up a rapport with somebody. It's a very deep friendship occurs, because you're living together, you've been through…although all abuse is different, it's all the same in the end. It's destroyed you, almost. So you build up this very deep bond. (Rachel)

At times, however, supportive relationships among the women could falter and have a detrimental effect if discussions became 'stuck':

> Talking about something is definitely good, but then when you go into it too much and keep talking and keep talking about the same old things, sometimes that can be a bit…sort of takes you back, really. And you can't really move on for it. You seem to be either just stuck in that certain moment, where you're just living all the time what he did. Which isn't always easy to break out of. (Jenny)[2]

From their own experience, women felt that it was far more difficult to give and receive support, or to get to know other women, both in self-contained accommodation and in larger communal refuges, unless management and/or workers actively planned settings and activities which could foster this. In particular, refuges with self-contained accommodation normally required women with children to remain with them once they were in bed, because of health and safety risks. This could limit the opportunities for the type of late-night support which appears to be characteristic of communal refuges. Amalie talked of feeling lonely:

> Here, I'm stuck. I feel isolated. Basically, having nobody to talk to. Yeah, there are other women in here with the same problem…but…we very rarely see them, because we have our own little flats. And you just get on with whatever you need to do that day and that's it. It's very rare you see any of the other women around. I mean, you pass them in the laundry, or if the kids are out playing on a sunny day you may see the mothers just bobbing down, see how the kids are. Things like that.

Even in favourable circumstances, it was not always possible for women to build a supportive network among themselves. There might not be women present that they could relate to, or small groups, which excluded others, might form. Each resident would also have her own pressing concerns, issues and agendas, which needed her attention and time if she was going to be able to leave the refuge and rebuild her life, so there might be less time available to support other women. Mutual support, then, although a valued and important resource, could not meet all the needs for communication and emotional support.

Worker support

Access to and interaction with workers was, therefore, very important to all the women, not just in considering specific courses of action or future plans, but in casual conversation about local or national events. This helped women who were experiencing acute emotional distress and facing difficult practical decisions to feel 'grounded' within everyday life and experiences. These conversations, which might also develop into supportive or healing talk, often occurred in the early evening when the children were in bed, no more active work required to be done and women could talk quietly to workers on a one-to-one basis, something that was not always possible during a working day. Kim, working a 'twilight shift', saw this as a valuable part of her work:

> More so in the evenings, women will come down to the office just for a chat. You know, they'll come down just to pick up their post and end up sitting and talking to us for half an hour, or sometimes even longer. And that's nice, because then we get to know them a bit more on a personal level as well, not just about issues that are going on for them. They could just be talking about, I don't know, a family member's having a birthday party, something like that…something nice going on, or a bargain they saw down in Asda. That's nice, for them to be able to come in and talk to us about those things as well. Things that are not necessarily about their issues around domestic violence, or what they've escaped. But just like everyday things.

Women appreciated the fact that generally they were able to go and talk to workers when they encountered problems or were in need of practical or emotional support; that wherever possible workers would make time to listen and, if necessary, would remain outside scheduled hours, or telephone to check that a problem had been resolved. They also valued the way workers understood the conflicting emotional and practical pressures they were subject to, as Jenny explained:

> It's just…I think they're a bit more…they really know that sometimes, you know, you do feel shit and sometimes you do need a little bit extra, sort of, time or, other times you can feel very positive and it just goes up and down like that. It's just that they know from their experience, even though everybody is different.

This support was not, however, always as readily available as either women or workers would have liked. Residents commented that the times they felt most isolated, whether in self-contained or communal accommodation, were out of hours – evenings and weekends – when workers had gone home. None of the refuges had scheduled full weekend staffing and were not in favour, at the time I visited, of 'sleep-ins' (i.e. where an on-duty worker is sleeping on the premises), seeing these as taking away responsibility from residents. During these times direct telephone access to workers was always available and women were also aware of Women's Aid and other helplines that they could contact. There was no evidence that these were extensively used. Indeed, there was a strong feeling that workers ought not to be 'bothered', if at all possible, during their off-duty hours, since they needed time and space to themselves and with their families after the intensity of the refuge work. Friday afternoons, before the weekend break, and Mondays, after workers returned, were inevitably particularly busy periods in all the refuges and there were times when women were unable to get the access they felt they needed. Barbara was only half in jest when she commented: 'Don't threaten suicide on a Monday, have to wait till Wednesday!' At other times, access might be restricted because of a number of new arrivals, pressure of administrative work within the refuge, meetings outside the refuge, or telephone calls. Handing over from one worker to another or checking arrangements for the day were other occasions when the office door might be closed and frustration among the women begin to mount.

Although women were well aware that refuges were under-resourced and that workers were under considerable pressure, not being able to make contact in this way was immensely frustrating and they felt angry and unsupported at these times, whether or not they had specific issues to discuss:

> I mean, the refuge workers are, basically, rushed off their feet. I mean, they have got a lot of commitments elsewhere…other women coming in and

out of the refuge. And we all…come 10 o'clock in the morning, there's a queue of people out there [outside the office door] waiting for calls, waiting for this, waiting for that. (Amalie)

Someone to listen

Interactions among the residents and between women and workers provided the main avenues of everyday conversation, practical information and emotional support and their importance was recognised and appreciated, despite the difficulties and frustrations that could occur from time to time. There was also, however, a desire, almost a yearning, for someone to be available to listen to their deepest concerns. This was often expressed as 'someone to talk to' or 'someone just for me'. Women felt that there were some aspects of their situation that they preferred to keep private from workers, but wanted to talk in confidence to someone who would understand the complexities of domestic violence, took the same sort of approach as the refuge workers, but could be seen as independent. Workers understood and appreciated this, aware that they were seen as being in a position of authority and that it was not necessary, or appropriate, for them to seek to cross boundaries and become aware of more private matters. They saw any supportive contacts residents might make as being complementary to the personal support and advocacy they provided and as offering a broader network of support systems.

A number of women had family or friends not too far away from the refuge. Some of these were willing to offer support, either in person or by telephone; others, for a variety of reasons, did not wish to get involved. Women were, in any case, reluctant to expose other members of their family to the potential risk of violence or intimidation from their abuser, or feared that he might be led inadvertently to the town or city where they were. There was always also the feeling that these supporters would have other concerns to attend to and that their goodwill should not be stretched too far. Women might feel able to talk to health workers or other visitors to the refuge, but were generally strongly in favour of counselling being readily available for any woman who wanted it, both while they were in the refuge and after they had left. Amy felt that it would be of benefit to many women: 'I think that counselling should be on offer. Because a lot of them that come in here, I know I did, I blamed myself for everything. But, I dunno…someone to talk to.'

Counselling[3]

Neither workers nor counsellors felt that formal counselling was appropriate or helpful when women first arrived at the refuge and were experiencing the shock and distress of the *Reception* phase discussed in Chapter 2. Once they had begun to move forward into the *Recognition* phase outlined in Chapter 3, workers felt that counselling could prove a valuable resource for those women who were ready for it, and that they were then able to support women as they gained new understandings:

> If a woman is ready for it, counselling is, it seems to me, the seat of where a woman can explore her stuff and see it slightly differently. You know, bounce back from the counsellor and everything. And then we can work with that, as she begins to move on, to see things slightly differently, to start feeling differently about herself and her place in the world. We can offer lots of support around that. (Daphne, worker)

In two of the refuge groups, counselling was available within the refuge at no cost to the resident. One group had a number of part-time counsellors together with a full-time paid counsellor, who also acted as a practice supervisor to the volunteer counsellors. In the other, a part-time volunteer counsellor visited on a regular basis. In the third group, part-time paid staff, together with volunteers, provided extensive counselling services. These were, however, at a centre some distance from the refuge and those residents who would have liked counselling felt that their other commitments, plus childcare arrangements, made it difficult for them to travel. (This may also be a reflection of their fears about safety when away from the refuge.)

Counsellors themselves followed a variety of theoretical perspectives, but had all received training in understanding the complex nature of domestic violence and its impact on women. Their aim was not to place responsibility for the violence on to the woman, but help her talk it through, mourn her loss and understand the relationship and her role in it so that she would be stronger on a personal and psychological level and less likely to be vulnerable in any future relationships. They agreed with workers that counselling was best seen as complementary to other support systems and part of an integrated package of refuge support, to be accessed as and when a woman wished to do so.

Of those residents who were eligible and had easy access to counselling, half were currently working with a counsellor. They made it clear that this was not, by any means, an easy option, but felt that it was helping them to understand themselves and what had happened to them and that it would benefit them in the future. Liz spoke freely about how counselling was changing her outlook:

> I have moved on…I have moved on, I've…I mean I've had…I've only had three sessions of counselling and…I thought about things I've not thought about for years. Things I don't *want* to think about, sometimes, as well, but I've thought about them and they've just come into my head and I think, wow, I must be ready, I must be ready to talk about them things. And I

found myself a strong person. I'm not emotional at all, but just over the last couple of months I've been like…because I want to talk, but not… I weren't ready. But like over the last three months I've like, I've not, I've not cared whether I look soft or whether I cry or whatever, like that. And I think it's a good thing that I'm coming out because otherwise it would just…I'd have ended up bitter and twisted, probably.

This one-to-one counselling was not for everyone. Two residents had tried a few sessions, but had felt it was not for them at present. Leanne was one of them: 'I tried that, but it wasn't for me. I think I'm better off just forgetting about it and talking about it, you never forget about it. I can pick it up later, when I'm ready for it.'

The possibility of obtaining some type of counselling after they had left the refuge was also mentioned by women who had no wish to enter counselling at present themselves, but wanted it to be available for others. The value of continuing or starting counselling was confirmed by ex-residents, two-thirds of whom had been in counselling during their stay and had returned for further sessions with the same counsellor after leaving the refuge. They commented that counselling had been helpful to them in both instances, but that the sessions after leaving had built on the earlier work. They were able to bring different aspects of their lives and problems into the frame and a much greater depth of understanding. Harriet commented: 'It's only really now that I've been able to get everything I need from counselling, if you see what I mean. Because I'm more settled and I know what I need to talk about.' The remaining two ex-residents had, like Leanne, continued to find individual counselling too painful, but had become involved in group work after they had left the refuge and found this very helpful and more useful for them than one-to-one sessions. Charmian said: 'The group was excellent. You could spark off each other, work together. It gave me confidence to try practical ways to change things.'

Counselling in the refuge setting presented specific challenges to counsellors. The lack of confidence and self-esteem so evident among women who had experienced domestic violence meant that counsellors needed to be more 'user friendly' – not simply coming to the refuge for an hour and departing, but taking time to be around and chat informally, but without crossing professional boundaries. This conveyed the message to residents, as one counsellor, Cara, put it, 'that people can trust me and know that I'm approachable and that I have got time for them'. It was also difficult for client and counsellor to build up the relationship of trust and rapport in which work could be carried out during the time spent in the refuge since both parties were aware that the temporary nature of the stay meant that the sessions might be abruptly terminated, perhaps giving rise to further feelings of loss. Despite these difficulties, it was apparent that a high proportion of women had found counselling of assistance at some stage in their journey of recovery and all of them were of the opinion that it needed to be made available in addition to the other services in the refuge.[4]

It was interesting to note that many of the volunteer counsellors were at an advanced stage of their professional training and were on placement from their colleges. Although they might have been expected to move on from the refuge after qualifying, those I spoke to expressed a firm commitment to this work and its value and hoped to continue to work in the refuge if they could possibly afford to do so.

Therapeutic group work[5]

Although counselling is becoming an accepted and established aspect in a growing number of refuges, therapeutic groups are a comparatively new concept in this setting. One viewpoint is that although they may prove helpful at a later date, they may be inappropriate for women while they are living in the refuge because of the crisis nature of their situation at this period of their lives.

At a refuge where one of the workers had a background and qualifications in psychiatry and counselling, a closed therapeutic group for survivors of sexual abuse had been developed. This ran at a separate location outside the refuge and included women both from the refuge and from the surrounding area. Additionally, an open therapeutic group followed the house meeting each week and this aimed particularly to deal with conflict resolution and develop confidence, as the facilitator, Cara, explained:

> It's loose group therapy. So if anyone wanted to leave, they could. But it's an area where women can look at the sort of dynamics that can come from living in multi-occupancy, but also about conflict resolution and that's really important, because, you know, if someone was sharing my kitchen, I wouldn't be too happy about it. And so it's all about sort of domestic stuff going on. But a lot of women have never had a positive resolution to a conflict, and for it to happen in the safety of a group can be really confidence building and it allows other people to see how conflict can be resolved peacefully but respectfully.

Some of the service users who attended these groups had found them challenging and hard work, but very rewarding. In particular, they felt that the open group had enabled them to learn how to deal with conflict resolution in a positive way and within a supportive environment. Others, however, had not felt comfortable with this way of working, feeling that they did not want to discuss individual problems and difficulties with other residents in front of other people.

Another of the refuge groups involved in this study had run, jointly with another project, an experimental closed self-help group with a therapeutic content for women who had experienced domestic violence (but who were not currently in the refuge) together with those who had experienced sexual abuse. Feedback from participants had been good, but it was not certain if resources would be available to run further groups or extend this work into the refuge. Evaluation of a number of other support and self-help groups with a therapeutic content[6] has shown that these were generally appreciated and seen as empowering by participants. However, these groups were not run within a refuge and this seems to tie in with Charmian's comments earlier in this chapter on the benefits of group work after leaving the refuge. Women who are still resident can, however, experience some of the benefits of a group by taking part in activities and workshops organised within the refuge.

Life skills and activities

For many people, work, training, or education provide an important arena for interaction and communication with others, as well as offering mental stimulation. It was much more difficult for women living in the refuge to access this resource and a constant comment, from ex-residents and residents alike, concerned the lack of activities to occupy their time, particularly during the day:

> It's frustrating, because…it's like, sometimes I'll get up in the morning, I'll take Debbie [daughter] to school. Then I've nowt to do and then we're either just sat in the kitchen, 'cup of teaing it' all day, or we're in us room and I think, oh God, there's got to be more to life than this. It's just thinking…ooh…I need more; I need to be doing more. (Liz)

Although this frustration was common to most of the women, it was particularly noticeable in those who, like Liz, had given up jobs on coming to the refuge. They and other women whose family commitments would have allowed it would have liked to work, but were caught in the job/rent/benefits trap whereby obtaining paid work resulted in a much higher rent and the cutting off of a range of benefits. Only well-paid jobs could overcome this loss and these were either not available or women lacked the necessary experience or qualifications to apply for them. Liz had also tried to obtain voluntary work, but had felt potential employers were stigmatising her, both because of her experience of domestic violence and because she was living in a refuge.[7]

The ability of all the women to finance activities for themselves and their children was severely curtailed by a level of benefits which had also to cover expenditure on food, clothing and replacing possessions which had had to be left behind, and which put even reduced college fees beyond them.

At all of the refuges, workers tried to provide activities for residents when resources were available to do so.[8] They saw these as a way of encouraging bonding, friendship and mutual support, particularly in refuges where self-contained accommodation made it more difficult to mix informally. It also enabled women to build confidence and develop life skills which would provide a valuable preparation for the time when they would move on and live independently.[9] At one refuge, weekly activity sessions were co-ordinated and facilitated by qualified workers from another section of the organisation. Elsewhere, arrangements were more ad hoc, including some events run by former residents who had revived old skills or learnt new ones. Topics ranged from beauty treatments and reflexology to first aid, alcohol information, child protection issues and benefits guidance and also provided a forum for discussions on managing money, general relationship issues and assertiveness. Creative art work, in particular, was credited by many of the workers as having helped women to express hidden feelings safely and learn from this experience.

These activities served several functions, as Danielle, one of the specialist group workers, explained: 'I suppose it's in three sections, really. Information, having fun and then more therapeutic stuff, you know, building up their confidence and self-esteem.' The informality of the groups made it easier to learn without being aware of doing so – as one of the refuge workers, Janna, commented: 'It's like a play club for adults.' Even when only a few women attended each session, residents and ex-residents who had taken part in some type of activity had found it excellent, saying that it had given them a chance to get together informally and have fun. They also felt that they were able to achieve something positive, which built up their self-esteem and confidence. Janet, a former resident, who showed me beautiful examples of her craftwork, remembered how she had discovered that she had this talent and what fun the group had been: 'We had some good laughs. I'm not very good at things like that. I'm surprised I can do it. Yeah, it was good.'

Going out as a group was also seen by women as a way in which they could have fun while developing new skills, building self-esteem and gaining the ability to handle situations confidently. As they pointed out, fears over safety and lack of confidence could make it difficult to do things as individuals, or even in pairs, whereas going out on a formal activity as a group, perhaps initially with worker support, overcame these difficulties. Other research[10] has seen this outside activity as being particularly important for many minority community women, who have often not been allowed to participate in any way in activities outside the family home and need to develop confidence in their own ability to do this.

Mothers and some women who did not have children with them, or whose families had grown up, had participated in a number of the outings arranged for children and had enjoyed these. Some had also been able to take part in trips without their children to nearby markets, or to the cinema, finding this both enjoyable and helpful in rebuilding social skills. Providing more of these opportunities was high on the 'wish list' of the majority of residents and former residents, but they were well aware of the constraints of time and money that refuges were working under.

Being a family

Women who had children with them in the refuge talked of the damage that domestic violence had done to the relationship between them and their children and of the need they felt to be able to talk and listen to each other. Many mothers had a clear understanding and concern for the fact that their children were going through as deep an emotional trauma as they were themselves. As Val pointed out: 'especially with the circumstances that they're in here, they're not…they're a bit emotionally unstable at the minute…their emotions are all over the place.' Play sessions were recognised as about far more than just play, but about helping them to cope with the new situation. Leanne, whose difficulties with her young son were mentioned earlier, was well aware of this deeper objective: 'The kids need it. Because they've seen enough and…they don't realise it, but when they get in on a play session it's like a counselling thing as well.'

Because women themselves were confronting difficult practical and emotional issues, they were not always able to respond to the concerns and needs of their children. Children's workers and volunteers were often able to bridge this gap and women said that they sometimes found it was easier to go and talk to these workers about other issues that were worrying them as well. Both refuge workers and children's workers were fully aware of this and suggested that it was probably because they were not seen as holding authority in the same way. The children's workers, such as Ellen, saw this willingness to talk to them as an important element in gaining trust and working with mothers on topics which helped the family as a whole:

> I do stuff with children after school and I think often the women will say 'Do you want a cup of coffee?' so I can go down and talk, chat…and in that way, often what they're wanting you to chat about is their children, sort of ways of doing things. So I feel I can offer support without being didactic about it. Being a parent is incredibly difficult.

In this informal atmosphere, it seemed to be easier for mothers to accept advice on parenting,[11] child development and how they, as well as the child workers, could work with their child or children. Several women talked to me about their own experiences of parenting and being parented, and their feeling that they had lacked a role model to help them learn these skills. They described as 'brilliant' the way child workers had shown them how they could work on themselves to relearn the responses they made to their children and how to understand and parent them.[12] This had had a major impact on them, given them a feeling of more control over their lives and the realisation that they could be proactive instead of reactive to events, an understanding which might well be carried forward into other situations. Clodagh explained why this work was so important in helping the mother and her children move forward and develop as a family:

> If the children are happy, then mums are happy too and vice versa. And they grow together. They need to grow together. Like mums grow, so do their children grow. We help a lot of mums with their parenting skills and things like that when they first come in, because they've had so much to deal with that their heads are jumbled up, that it's hard for them to take a step back and think about the children and things like that because they've got so many different things on in their mind. It's good, because they both grow together, which is really nice. Nice seeing them as family units and doing things together.

During the time I spent in each refuge, I could see for myself just how important it was to women to be able to reach out and communicate with others and the many ways in which they did so. The interviews themselves provided yet another opportunity for this to happen and, as women came to accept me, they also involved me in informal discussions, added comments to what they had said in the interviews and put forward new ideas. Formal and informal feedback showed that they had valued the opportunity to make further connections and give a voice to their views.

Summary

- The isolation imposed on women by their abusers had resulted in an intense need for communication and interaction with other people, once they were in a safe place. This need to reach out to others and connect to a community has been identified by Maslow (1987) as one of the basic needs of human beings. (See Chapter 1 for a fuller discussion of this.)

- Women identified this contact as being needed on three levels: everyday conversation, supportive talk and the healing talk which enabled them to reflect on their experiences and learn to deal with their emotional distress. These levels were not clearly separable and women drew on a variety of sources to piece together a network of communication and support.

- Residents in communal refuges were able to exchange experiences, learn from each other and discuss political and social issues. This was more difficult in self-contained accommodation, unless specifically planned for by workers.

- The availability of mutual support was dependent on the 'mix' of residents and their own concerns at any one time. It was also possible that women could become 'stuck' in discussions about the abuse and find it difficult to move on.

- Women appreciated the time that workers spent with them, both formally and informally, and their understanding of the stresses they experienced. At times, however, under-resourcing and pressure of work meant that less support was available to meet women's needs and this resulted in feelings of anger and frustration.

- Family or friends might be willing to offer support to residents, either by telephone or meeting them, but women were often reluctant to involve them, for fear of repercussions or because they did not wish to impose further burdens on those who had other concerns to deal with.

- Women wanted to be able to talk in confidence to someone who understood the complexities of domestic violence and who would take time to listen to their deeper concerns. They felt strongly that counselling should be readily available within the refuge for those women who wanted it, together with the option of accessing counselling once they had left the refuge. The opportunity to participate in self-help and other group work after leaving was also thought to be a valuable service.

- Counsellors needed to be seen as independent of the refuge organisation, but sharing the same values and to be approachable, while maintaining professional boundaries. Counselling in the refuge situation, because of the possibility of early termination, presented special problems in building a therapeutic relationship in which work could be done.

- Access to training, work, or education while in the refuge was severely limited due to benefit levels and regulations. This also made it difficult for women to finance other activities for themselves and their children.

- Group activities were seen as a way of building confidence and self-esteem, helping informal support networks to develop and enabling women to learn skills that would be of help when they had left the refuge and were living independently.

- Mothers understood that their children were undergoing acute emotional distress, but because of their own difficulties were not always able to offer appropriate reactions. The role of children's workers in bridging this gap, working with both children and their mothers was deeply valued.

Notes

1. This has been a recurring feature in both early and later research accounts (McGee 2000a; Rose 1985).

2. Feeling pressure from other residents to keep talking when women wanted to move on or needed space was also noted by Rai and Thiara (1997). The risk of 'getting stuck' in this way might be less problematic in second stage or 'move on' accommodation. This type of accommodation is generally in short supply and was not available to the groups involved in this research.

3. Counselling is used here to describe a formal, explicit and agreed relationship between two people to meet in private at set times, within clear boundaries and with a mutual understanding of confidentiality, to work on specific aims connected with self-understanding and personal growth (Bond 2000; British Association for Counselling and Psychotherapy 2002). Counsellors are usually trained and belong to a professional body with a code of ethics to which they are expected to adhere.

4. Counselling has been seen as running counter to a feminist analysis of domestic violence, by focusing on the personal inadequacy of the woman and adopting a 'victim blaming' approach, rather than exploring the problem of violent men and an unequal society. Although there is still some controversy over counselling, feminist approaches have now emerged (Coleman and Guildford 2001; Whalen 1996) and a high proportion of Women's Aid refuges now offer counselling. Research (Lodge, Goodwin and Pearson 2001; McGee 2000b; Rai and Thiara 1997) has shown that this is a service requested and appreciated by past and current residents.

5. Therapeutic groups are designed to enable individuals who have shared similar problems to explore together the difficult experiences in their lives and deal with their feelings in a safe and supportive environment (Arnold and Magill 2000). Facilitators will normally have training in and experience of this work and a background in counselling or psychotherapy. A closed group will not enrol further members after the group has started to run. In an open group, people who have shared similar experiences may join or leave at any stage and the group may have no finite end. Because of the changes in participants, it may be less intense than a closed group, but equally require appropriate skills and abilities to facilitate. Self-help or support groups operate in a wide range of situations and are designed to enable members to support each other, share understanding and gain strength and awareness in the process (Butler and Wintram 1991; Mullender and Ward 1991).

6. Batsleer *et al.* (2002); Hester and Westmarland (2005).

7. Also noted by McGee (2000a). It is possible that this may also, on the part of employers, be due to some extent to their awareness of the transitory nature of refuges.

8. Arranging these activities took considerable time and effort, particularly if it involved bringing in outside agencies who would only participate if a guaranteed number of women took part. By the time the activity was arranged, those who had originally suggested it might well have moved on, have other preoccupations or, because of their emotional situation, not want to join the group.

9. Similar findings come from Charles (1994) and Rai and Thiara (1997).

10. Batsleer *et al.* (2002). This was also an issue stressed in personal communication by workers from a specialist Asian refuge. Butler and Wintram (1991) confirm this view of group trips out, arguing that they involve both fun and risk taking and provide scope for the development of trust and personal growth.

11. Although all the comments I received on children's workers and the development of parenting skills were positive and enthusiastic, it must be remembered that parenting is an extremely sensitive area, with attitudes shaped by a variety of influences, including class, age and ethnicity. Women are unlikely to readily accept interference when dealing with their children and it is possible, therefore, that women who took a different approach to that of the refuge would not have stayed in this environment long, or might not have been willing to be interviewed.

12. All of the residents and ex-residents interviewed, whether they had had children with them at the time of their stay or not, were unanimous in their appreciation of the knowledge and skills of the children's workers and volunteers and the work that was carried out with children, in particular, the activities organised for children during the week and in the school holidays.

Chapter 5

Living Together

It is the refuge itself that provides the background to the daily life of its residents, offering safe accommodation, the opportunity to connect to other people and to access the emotional and practical support which fosters the growth of self-esteem and confidence. Within this environment, women can work through the process of grieving and gradual recovery from the losses that domestic violence has inflicted on them.

Not surprisingly, the refuge, its organisation and day-to-day management were topics of great importance to women, who were eager both to express their opinions and to offer their ideas for improvements. They had strong views on many aspects of the subject; on the relative merits and drawbacks of communal and self-contained accommodation, on what refuges should be like, on conflict and tensions and how they saw their role in the running of the refuge. In expressing these opinions, they drew on their experiences of small and large refuges throughout England, of different types of accommodation and operational regimes. Their comments both confirm past research and offer fresh insights into refuge life and what women seek in terms of refuge provision.

Daily life

Sharing kitchens, living space and, in emergencies, bedrooms with other families has been a feature of refuge life in Women's Aid since its inception, although this pattern is now beginning to change with the growth of purpose built refuges.[1] Suddenly being plunged into close association with a varied group of women could come as a shock, as Barbara described:

> It's weird when you first experience that, yes. I mean, suddenly, you've got to get on with other people. You've had your own space and you've had just one person, if it's your husband who's living with you…you're used to daily mental and physical battles with one person. You just have to deal with

one person, and kids, as well, perhaps, if you're younger. But not being used to all these other women…and suddenly, they're all there!

There was a common understanding that the close proximity of families and the stress of the different emotional and practical problems that each individual was dealing with meant that the smallest incident could become a major source of friction unless there was a considerable degree of tolerance from everyone involved, as Jenny explained:

> You're living in each other's pockets, which is obvious. And it's not people that… You, maybe, wouldn't choose the ones that you live with. But, with it being all sorts of different people, like I said before, you do learn, really, to adjust…We fit round each other, because there's no point in, sort of, picking at the little things that maybe you would do different, or they would do different. It's just easier.

And Stacey saw no point in bickering: 'We just laugh. And if we didn't laugh, we'd cry. And, sometimes, you can't afford to cry.'

Sharing a kitchen with other women has the potential to be extremely diffi-cult and women agreed that it could be chaotic there at times, particularly at weekends, or holiday times, or when the children came home from school, all wanting their tea, with both cooking facilities and space at a premium. But kitchens were also seen as places to sit and talk, or work together and they could also be the venue for joyful communal meals on special occasions. Charmian recalled cooking a Christmas dinner for five women and ten children, and women at other refuges talked of joint birthday parties and of the pleasure of sharing other meals with fellow residents.

In line with the policy of seeing the refuge as being 'home' to a family, house rules were kept to the minimum felt necessary to observe health and safety regula-tions and any other statutory responsibilities, and to respect the refuge, workers, volunteers and other residents. Although women fully understood and appreci-ated the need for house rules, at times they found them frustrating and irritating, particularly when they were different from the standards and behaviour that would have been customary at home. Women who had been in the refuge for some time commented that even restrictions that they accepted as very necessary became more and more irksome as time passed and they saw little prospect of moving out. For women with children, house rules on bedtime, behaviour and supervision could be problematic to enforce when these were different from those that the children had previously understood. Different methods of upbringing could also cause friction within the family, as children challenged why they had to behave in certain ways, or weren't allowed to do things other children did.

By far the biggest source of friction in communal refuges was the requirement to clean the family space and to share in the cleaning of communal areas, including kitchens, toilets and bathrooms. Women had widely different expectations of the standards of cleanliness which should be maintained, the frequency of cleaning and views on the extent to which other women were 'doing their share'. It was the topic most often commented on in no uncertain terms to me and the one which workers said was most often raised in house meetings, as it appears to have been in all previous research and from my informal conversations with former workers.[2]

Away from communal areas, the need to share a family room with their children could restrict personal space and privacy for all concerned:

> The problem most mothers, especially with older children, have is that they're in the same room as their children. You have no privacy. Say it's your time of the month, or you want to write a letter, or something, your children are there. They're there and you can't get away from that. There's absolutely no privacy for a mother to, perhaps, shave her legs, or, as I say, time of the month and things like that. It's difficult if you've got a son of 11, or something. (Rachel)

Stacey, sharing a room with her 14-year-old daughter, said it wasn't easy for either of them:

> It's…are you going to do me a bacon sandwich, Mum? Are you going to depart the bedroom while I get up and washed? And dressed? Do you have to have your radio on? Because I'm trying to do maths. I don't like them curtains open, Mum, can't we have them shut?

Women were very realistic and frank about the physical disadvantages and restrictions of communal living, but came back time and again to constantly reiterate the fact that they now felt safe and supported within a community. In assessing the advantages and disadvantages of living together, they balanced the difficulties against the major benefits they felt could be gained from being with other women – companionship, emotional support, understanding and, above all, the connections to others:

> Yeah, you're living on top of somebody else, but it's like…being a family again. You're not as isolated. If the other women have got children, fair enough, then you muck in, tidy up. Everybody does their bit, they all pull together. (Amalie)

> When you've been through domestic violence, the last thing you want is to be on your own. But here, you've got the choice. You can go to your bedroom and be on your own, or you can sit in the living room with everybody else. So…but I think your kitchen should be shared, because otherwise you just go and lock yourself away and brood on it and get stressed out. It's not good for you. (Leanne)

Those women who were currently in a refuge with self-contained accommodation (i.e. rooms or flats with their own cooking and toilet facilities), or had previously experienced this level of provision, very much appreciated the additional facilities this gave them, in particular, having their own family space together with privacy for themselves. The big disadvantage, in their opinion, was the difficulty of interaction with other women and the feelings of isolation and detachment that this could lead to, as Amy had found: 'In here, you could see somebody one day and then you might not see anyone for, like, three days. That person. You know. And then, like, negativity.' Shelley had not been in this type of refuge before:

> The people here, I've met them, but nobody's...I don't think mixes, only when there's a group, or something. Everybody seems to keep themselves to themselves, if you know what I mean. They're...whether they're a bit worried or scared or, you know...which it is frightening in here, sometimes. I think that's why everyone keeps themselves to themselves.

Workers felt that self-contained accommodation provided the quality and privacy that women needed and deserved, but were also aware that if a woman did not access the communal areas or come to the office, extra effort needed to be made to ensure that she was receiving all the support she needed, without appearing to intrude unduly. Group activities and events (as discussed in the previous chapter) provided opportunities for women to talk together, but if women lacked confidence it might be difficult for them to access these facilities without specific encouragement. In these circumstances, ways to facilitate women meeting together and talking to each other needed to be carefully developed and fostered.

Conflict

Given the stresses and tensions of refuge life and the underlying feelings of loss, anger and unpredictable emotional turbulence which all the women experienced, some form of conflict between residents will inevitably surface at some point, however much tolerance is exercised by everyone concerned. Such episodes can have a major effect on residents and communal life, as Jay, a worker with many years experience, commented: 'When it works for women, it really, really works. It can be very supportive. When it doesn't, it's bloody awful!'

As well as the work they carried out with individual women and families, in terms of practical and emotional support, workers saw their role within the refuge setting as supporting women to live co-operatively, and to handle the strains and tensions of communal living.[3] Their aim was to get residents to deal with internal conflicts by themselves, in order to help them to develop the skills of assertiveness and negotiation that they would need once they had left the refuge. They were, however, available for matters that residents felt unable to deal with face to face, or to intervene if they became aware that there was a major problem. Difficulties could also be taken to house meetings, where they could be discussed openly by women and workers. A few women from each refuge welcomed this responsibility, seeing it as an opportunity to 'stand up for themselves' and try out new skills:

> If you're not happy with someone else, then that's the time to say. I think it's good in a way, because you've got to learn to stick up for yourself, really. Be strong. It's a way of learning. For me it is, anyway. (Eve)

Other women, however, did not feel ready, or willing, to tackle problems openly and felt uncomfortable and distressed if internal differences were aired in joint meetings with workers. In all the refuges, there were certain issues that women felt unwilling to raise among themselves, nor did they wish to take them to the workers, or bring them up at house meetings. Sometimes these were matters that women felt were inevitable and just had to be put up with, such as personality clashes or the formation of small groups among residents, but there were also times when women felt that they had been 'bossed around', 'picked on' or discriminated against by other women because of some perceived difference like 'talking posh'[4] or having a different way of doing things.

Part of the reluctance to take problems like these to the workers sprang from the way they were perceived by women. Despite the efforts they made to work in partnership with women and create equal relationships, workers were aware that they were seen as being in a position of authority – collecting rents, enforcing rules, issuing warnings, possibly dealing with child protection issues:

> Women's perceptions of refuge workers can be quite…well, you know, refuge workers are in a position where they're…they're the people that enforce rules, fundamentally. They've got a lot of power, refuge workers. We've got a lot of power. And we have to enforce rules. We are the ones who are nagging you for your rent and nagging you because you left the back door open and having a go because your children are unsupervised. (Jay, worker)

> It does tend to be us and them, maybe it shouldn't be, but it is, because the workers, the staff here are, they're in a position of kind of, not so much control, but in a way it is, really. I mean, they can say yes to stuff, you know, things that we can and can't do. (Barbara, resident)

Given these perceptions, going to the workers with issues like these might be seen as 'sneaking' to authority. As Rachel commented: 'It's almost like children not telling their mums, or something.' It might also involve revealing their own fears and crossing personal boundaries of privacy and vulnerability. Additionally, there appeared to be a common feeling among residents that they did not want to 'cause trouble' for women in a similar situation to their own, unless it became clear that the resident concerned was a major threat to the security of the refuge, or her behaviour was considered unacceptable by the majority of women. In these circumstances, as Amy said: 'You don't like to lose anyone their roof, but staff had to be told.'

In smaller refuges, if workers raised issues directly with residents or at house meetings, women pointed out that everyone was going to know who had taken this action and residents and ex-residents agreed that they preferred to 'put up with things' rather than risk losing the friendship and mutual support of other residents, as Charmian explained: 'I was frightened of speaking out, because I didn't want to lose the friends I'd made. And there might have been reprisals later on, when the workers had gone home.'[5]

Workers were aware of these fears and of the constant undercurrents and changes in the house dynamics which never quite surfaced, feeling that this mirrored, in some ways, the 'hidden' aspects of domestic abuse. Issues such as bullying and discrimination were discussed on arrival and it was made clear then and at subsequent house meetings that this was not considered to be acceptable behaviour. However, as they pointed out, if women were unable or unwilling to bring issues to them, it was difficult for them to identify the problem, or to frame appropriate interventions, even if this might have been possible or desirable.

Every change of resident affected the dynamics and atmosphere of the refuge and this could also be affected by the changing relationship among the workers or volunteers. Women were also quick to sense any tension or perceived conflict among them and would become anxious and fearful in consequence, sometimes wondering if this was something to do with them, or if they had caused problems in some way. This 'sixth sense' of impending difficulties was very highly developed among the women and had clearly been a way of coping with and surviving within the abusive relationship. To encounter similar difficulties within the refuge, then, was particularly distressing as it replicated the feelings of uncertainty and insecurity that women had experienced previously. Workers understood clearly the effects that this could have, as Jay commented: 'A dysfunctional staff team, ultimately, impacts on women more than anybody else.' Daphne emphasised the need to keep problems of this nature away from the direct contact with women:

> We have to recognise that what we do and what we say, whether it's in front of our kids, or in front of the women, it's bouncing back on us and, you know, we have to look at that. I mean, there were a couple of incidents a few weeks ago and the women were very unhappy. You know, that kitchen cleared so quickly it was like there had been a bomb announcement. One minute it's full – and half an hour later – they've gone! So it's about understanding the effects and how it affects the women.

Workers also talked of the need to maintain their own boundaries and avoid bringing too many details of their personal lives and problems into the refuge. Not only could this result in safety and security problems now or in the future, but women who were already burdened with their own problems might feel the need to take these concerns on board as well.

Participation

Early accounts of refuge life[6] show volunteers, a few paid workers and residents working together to clean and maintain the refuge and making joint decisions on admissions, eviction and general policy in weekly house meetings. Participation in every aspect of refuge life in this way is now very unlikely to take place, since the growth in administrative and legal requirements and the complexity of the social and welfare systems has meant that specialisation has become necessary to ensure up-to-date knowledge and expertise are available. Specialist services, including child support, counselling and outreach have also been developed, requiring additional training and qualifications. As a result, a more structured approach has developed, with mainly hierarchical systems and paid workers. All of the groups involved in this research had specialist finance and administrative staff and paid refuge workers who handled admissions and evictions, together with part-time housekeepers to attend to health and safety regulations, cleanliness and maintenance (although general and specialist workers and volunteers were fully prepared to assist in this if it became necessary). Housekeepers also controlled or drew up cleaning rotas, although women were responsible for cleaning their own rooms and a specified part of the communal areas.

In one group, attendance at weekly house meetings was a licence condition and at another it had become a cultural expectation. In the third group, with self-contained accommodation, meetings were less frequent and although well publicised were very poorly attended. One resident at this refuge suggested that women were just trying to get their heads round their problems and to cope with their immediate needs, so that for some of them attendance at meetings was just another burden they could do without. 'I don't know,' said Amalie, 'I think, basically, they're just getting on with their own lives. Just trapped in their own little worlds.'

The main subjects for discussion at the house meetings were cleaning and maintenance, additional requirements in the way of furniture and utensils and any planned renovations. Topics like security and licence conditions and any problems which had been reported to the staff would be talked about and residents might put forward suggestions for activities or improvements. Depending on the women in the refuge at the time, topics like discrimination and inequality might provoke a lively debate, but equally there might be no desire to discuss these issues. Despite the best efforts of workers, the conflicts and tensions discussed in the previous section were not always openly dealt with:

> But they still don't work with problems. Nobody says...at the house meetings, they just won't say it. Just something I'm trying to work on with them. So, usually, I'll get someone coming in before, to speak to me, will you bring this up? Which is fine, but then you get there and you bring it up and everybody just sits there with their mouths shut. It's just too intimidating, isn't it? (Katja)

Most residents appeared to take the view expressed earlier that paid workers were in a position of authority within the refuge and it was their responsibility to organise and make decisions. They felt that their immediate concerns were heard either through the house meetings, direct discussions with workers, suggestion boxes or regular confidential questionnaires. 'They listen to what we say,' said Val. They were, however, very dubious as to the extent to which they could actually influence or change policy.[7] Grievance procedures and ways of making a complaint were clearly set out and understood, although few women felt they would take action in this way, perhaps due to the fear that it might injure their relationships with workers or other women, or the feeling that it was just something else to be put up with. There seemed to be no real desire on the part of most residents to take a more active role in running the refuge. Leanne appeared to express the majority view in saying: 'We get enough...we gets what we needs.' A few women, on the other hand, did want to take part in decision making and were actively looking for a role for themselves. Liz, whose efforts to seek work were mentioned in Chapter 4, saw this as a way of building her confidence and capacity to act, which had been damaged by her experiences of domestic violence:

> It'd be a good thing, because you'd think you feel part of it, more. I don't know, just...being able to, being put in a position where you can arrange something and that'd be your little project. It could be anything, you know, just, like, organising a day out, or something like that. Actually feeling responsible and getting used to being responsible again. That would be a good thing. Because here...it's like, sometimes, you feel you can't think for yourself. So, like, you go in the office for pathetic, silly little things. Whereas, when you're in your own home, you wouldn't dream – you'd just go do it!

Workers in all the refuges were concerned to gain greater involvement and to raise the level and range of discussions and were actively engaged in investigating how to improve the position. As they commented, the refuge movement had started with residents, workers and volunteers working together. This had provided the impetus for growth and social change and was a valuable source of ideas and innovation, which needed to be tapped into. Additionally, there was now a growing emphasis on user participation and consumer involvement in current government thinking. Monthly questionnaires sent in confidence to the local management committee, exit questionnaires, suggestion boxes and informal coffee mornings to encourage discussion were some of the ideas which had been tried, as was placing items of particular interest to residents on the agenda of the house meetings. As Jay pointed out, however, if women chose not to use these options, there was no way in which participation could or should be imposed:

> Well, you're offering them, but women are not using them. What's that about? And is it that, actually, women don't want to be involved? Is it that they want to come in, eat, sleep and get rehoused? And have a say, maybe, once they've gone? I really do think that, for some women, they don't want to be involved. And there's so many other things going on for them that they…I'm not saying they don't do it, because there are other women who do want to be. For some women, they just don't want to know. And I think that's fair enough.

Daphne linked the limited participation to the broader issue of the type of alienation which has limited voting in recent years and to a general feeling of powerlessness within society. Her comments reflect the thoughts of those residents who had said to me that their views were unlikely to affect policy making:

> I don't think it's apathy, I think it's alienation, that people feel alienated from the whole decision-making, political processes that go on… People do feel alienated, they don't feel that they know what people are talking about, that they have any power to make any decisions or to change anything. So they just withdraw. They just vote with their feet. And that's possibly how the women might say, oh, it's nothing to do with us.

Service users were not represented on the management committees of any of the groups, although management committee members themselves may well have been women who had experienced domestic violence at some point in their lives. A wide variety of views was expressed by workers as to whether women living in the refuges should be represented on management committees. The general consensus seemed to be that it would be better to wait until a reasonable period after the woman had left the refuge since, while she was 'in the experience', the emotional stresses might create additional problems for her and adversely affect her ability to contribute to discussions.

While women were very aware of their emotional fluctuations, there were, nevertheless, a small number of strong and articulate women in all the refuges who, with adequate support and encouragement, would have been able, in my view, to make valuable contributions to these meetings and in other areas, such as focus groups and campaigning. Such participation would enable agencies to understand better the needs of women who have experienced domestic violence and provide opportunities for personal growth, but would need careful consideration to avoid the danger of a woman feeling used or exploited.[8]

Other experiences of refuge life

Eight of the women who talked to me had paid more than one visit to a refuge, and others had spent a few days or weeks in other refuges immediately prior to moving to one of the refuges in this project. Between them, they offered comments on stays in 26 other refuges. Women were rarely certain whether the refuges they went to were run by Women's Aid members or, in some cases, how many they had been to and exactly where they were. (This was most often the case when the visit had been short and the woman was in the state of shock, numbness and confusion which I have referred to as the *Reception* phase.) In general, praise and criticism mirrored the comments made about the refuges in the research project. Workers who provided an unhurried reception and respectful approach, explained options and offered emotional as well as practical support and time to talk to them were highly regarded. However, when women arrived in a refuge at the end of a working day and felt that workers wanted to deal with them as quickly as possible so that they could go home, this was experienced as disempowering and reinforcing feelings of worthlessness. Charmian commented: 'She was waiting to go home and kept saying "Is there anything else you need?" I felt I'd just been dumped there and left to get on with it.'

Some of the refuges that women had stayed in were clearly not affiliated to Women's Aid, since they offered only warden controlled accommodation. Although this was secure to an extent, women felt very unsupported[9] and unable to obtain the practical and emotional help they needed. This was also true of accommodation where there were too few workers for the size of the refuge. In general, it was the smaller communal refuges which were preferred, rather than the larger ones, or those with self-contained accommodation, which were both sometimes experienced as frightening and isolating:

> I didn't like that. There was too many of us...too many of us in one place. Too many. Quite frightening. (Eve)

> It was just, it was like an office building and there was just too many floors, too many rooms and...it just weren't nice at all. Commercialised. They had rooms, TV rooms where you could go, but they were on each floor, so, if you were on that floor, you all stayed there. There was nowhere for you to mix, or meet other people and that. And, like, you didn't see the staff. You just got up and you was in your room all the time. (Val)

While women acknowledged that some rules and regulations were necessary, both to ensure the security of the refuge and to facilitate refuge life, some of them had experienced workers in other refuges as dictatorial and controlling of their actions and behaviour, thus recreating the abusive behaviour they had come to the refuge to escape. Maryam talked of 'feeling like a criminal'[10] and that 'if you say anything they're gonna make your stay uncomfortable', while Amalie commented: 'You weren't allowed…you weren't allowed to have, basically, to have a life.'

In listening to these comments, I wondered if women were nervous, despite assurances of confidentiality, of voicing this sort of criticism in relation to the current refuge, in case it affected their relationship with the workers, and may, therefore, have chosen to project it on to their previous refuge stay. But I found throughout this research project that women did not seem inhibited in voicing criticism of their current refuge or staff in other directions (poor conditions, lack of activities, restricted access to workers) and although forceful comments were on occasion made 'off record', controlling behaviour on the part of workers was never mentioned.

How it could be

When women were asked to say what improvements they would like to see in refuge provision, the first response was always to provide good quality accommodation, which encouraged a degree of interaction with other residents and also gave easy access to workers. It was clear that this was regarded as a baseline which underpinned and could improve all the other forms of support available. Residents and ex-residents alike had strong views on the topic and brought in many of the points they had raised earlier in our conversations regarding mutual support and the pros and cons of communal or self-contained accommodation. Key provisions were:

- Quality accommodation. Many of the women in this study had come from well-established homes with good facilities. Living in poor accommodation increases their feelings of worthlessness and reinforced the impression that they were being punished for no fault of their own.

- Well maintained. Every new refuge is full from the moment it opens and no room stays vacant for long. Multiple occupancy and a changing population with large numbers of children creates additional wear and tear on both fabric and furnishings.

- Adequate security measures, including security cameras and alarm systems.

- Separate bedrooms to give mothers privacy from children.

- Some privacy for teenagers away from both parents and younger children.

- Own toilet and personal washing facilities.

- Shared kitchens, but with sufficient individual cooking facilities and space to minimise conflict. The main body of opinion was emphatically in favour of shared cooking and eating facilities, to provide opportunities for conversation and lessen isolation. A very small minority wanted their own cooking facilities (but not the restrictions this imposed concerning children's safety).

- Shared communal areas to encourage interaction, friendship and mutual support and provide a space for group activities.

- Quiet rooms for interviews or counselling. Some women wanted to see a specific area for prayer, meditation or quiet thought.

- Easy access to workers for practical and emotional support. Suggestions included providing a separate office with only one worker, to make it easier for women with low self-confidence who may find big offices intimidating, more 'twilight' working and increased weekend staffing. Opinion was divided as to whether 24-hour staffing was beneficial or not.

- Small family-sized refuges. Nine or more family rooms in a house was regarded as much too big by women who had experienced refuges of this size. They also pointed out that this would limit the numbers of children at any one time and reduce the inevitable noise levels, particularly at weekends and at holidays.

Women felt that this type of accommodation would give them more privacy, a quiet space to think and a better quality of life during their stay in the refuge, while providing the communal support and encouragement that they found invaluable and the opportunity to access the knowledge and skills of workers and volunteers. It was also an arrangement which might minimise occasions on which conflict might arise and encourage the growth of supportive networks.

In discussing provision for women and children with different needs (larger families, physical impairments, cultural differences and so on) particular mention was made of the needs for separate provision, with enhanced and specialist support, for women whose problems with domestic violence were associated with drug or alcohol dependencies, or mental health difficulties.[11] The scarcity of provision for people with limited physical mobility was also mentioned and one woman, who was herself dependent on a walking aid, felt that in these circumstances there was a case for 24-hour staffing, or some kind of alarm system.

Although refuge provision will differ in requirements for different parts of the country, there seem to be certain features common to all the research which has been carried out over the past two decades on the provision of accommodation for women leaving situations of domestic violence. These echo, without exception, the views of my informants, including the need for privacy, smaller, family-sized refuges, communal spaces and shared, adequate cooking facilities.[12] A survey of seven refuges across England by Delahay and Turner (1998) found that 65 per cent of women positively preferred to live with communal facilities over the isolation of self-contained accommodation.[13] However, local authorities and housing associations are showing a marked preference, both in purpose-built accommodation and conversions, for self-contained bed-sitting rooms or flats, both to provide better facilities for women and to enable premises to cater for other housing categories, such as workers in essential jobs with priority housing needs, at a later date. Larger units, which give added economies of scale, are also a preferred option.[14] Service users have expressed clear and consistent views for the past 20 years on the type of refuges that would best meet their requirements and these should be taken fully into account by funders and agencies in planning future accommodation and services, if women are to feel that their participation will genuinely make a difference to outcomes.

Summary

- The refuge provides the background for daily life, offering safe accommodation, the opportunity to connect to others and to access the practical and emotional support which fosters the growth of self-esteem and confidence. These factors, described by Maslow (1987) as basic to human need, create an environment in which women can work through the process of grieving and gradual recovery from the losses that domestic violence has inflicted on them.

- The close proximity of families and the stress of the emotional and practical difficulties they had to tackle meant that residents needed to exercise a considerable degree of tolerance and understanding in their dealings with each other. This was particularly so in communal refuges, but was also needed in self-contained accommodation.

- Differing standards of cleanliness and child rearing in cramped conditions and other women not 'doing their share' were sources of frustration and annoyance.

- Sharing a room together meant that there was a lack of privacy for mothers and children. This could be particularly difficult where adolescent children were involved.

- House rules were kept to the minimum necessary to comply with health and safety regulations and other statutory requirements and to ensure respect for the refuge environment, staff and other residents. It was not always easy, however, for residents to remember and observe these rules.

- Women were realistic about the physical disadvantages and restrictions of communal living, but emphasised the positive aspects: the companionship, strength support and understanding that they gained from other women. They saw the interaction and support between residents that was available in this situation as being a key element in recovering from their experiences.

- Self-contained accommodation was valued for the privacy and family space it gave, but could lead to isolation and detachment unless women were encouraged to participate in activities. Workers needed to ensure that women had the support they needed without appearing unduly intrusive.

- Warden controlled accommodation, although secure, did not offer the degree of practical and emotional support which women felt they needed.

- The aim of workers was to support women to live co-operatively and to deal with internal conflicts themselves, while being available to assist with more major problems. Where women were not willing to bring difficulties into the open, it was hard to identify conflicts and frame appropriate interventions. Any perceived conflict among workers would adversely affect the women in the refuge.

- Workers made every effort to tackle problems of discrimination and to ensure that women fully understood that this was not considered acceptable behaviour. Nevertheless, some forms of discrimination did take place among residents and this was not necessarily limited to members of minority ethnic groups.

- Workers were seen as being in positions of authority and responsible for organising and taking decisions. Women felt that they were listened to and consulted with, but that their views were unlikely to have any major effect on policy. Most of them did not feel inclined to participate further in running the refuge, although workers were actively trying to increase the level of involvement.

- A few residents did want to participate in decision making and would have liked to find a more active role for themselves. They would have much to offer to agencies and in campaigning, provided that adequate safeguards were in place to prevent any feelings of exploitation.

- Women felt that good quality, secure and well-maintained accommodation with a degree of privacy and family space needed to be available, preferably in small, family-sized refuges. Shared kitchens and other communal areas were seen as important to encourage interaction with other residents and mutual support, together with easy access to workers. It was clear that this was regarded as a baseline which underpinned and could improve all the other forms of support available.

Notes

1. Of the six refuge buildings run by the groups involved in this project, only one was a purpose-built block with 13 families in self-contained flats together with communal areas. The remainder were older properties for between three and six families, one of which had been converted into small bed-sits with cooking facilities and additional communal spaces, while the others were fully communal.

2. Batsleer et al. (2002); Binney et al. (1981); Charles (1994); Clifton (1985); Hoff (1990); Pahl (1978); Rai and Thiara (1997); Rose (1985).

3. Providing a containing role in this way, without constantly intervening, has always been a guiding principle of Women's Aid refuges (Clifton 1985; Harwin 1997).

4. Ball (1994) also comments on women feeling 'picked on' and bossed around by other residents. Discrimination on the grounds of race did not appear to be a major problem in any of the refuges, with women saying that they were more concerned with the standards of cleanliness and behaviour of children than ethnic origins. The only refuge where there was a significant number of minority community women, however, provided self-contained accommodation, which limited the opportunities for interaction and possible friction. Incidents of racist behaviour between residents and workers and residents were noted by Rai and Thiara (1997) and Batsleer et al. (2002). The latter also point out that discrimination is not limited to women normally considered to come from minority communities, but can also extend to other groups, such as Jewish or Irish women in mainstream refuges. One white British woman in my study, who had spent time in a predominantly Asian refuge, felt that she was being discriminated against by the other residents.

5. This fear was also noted by Rai and Thiara in their (1997) study.

6. Binney et al. (1981); Clifton (1985); Pahl (1978); Rose (1985).

7. Similar opinions were voiced to Delahay and Turner (1998) and Hague et al. (2002).

8. This view was also taken by Hague et al. (2002) who suggest that the existing practices need to be reviewed.

9. The lack of support in this type of accommodation was also noted by McGee (2000a).

10. Similar comments were made to Rai and Thiara (1997).

11. For a fuller discussion of these special needs see Chapter 2 and the research carried out by Barron (2004).

12. Binney et al. (1981); Charles (1994); McGee (2000a); Pahl (1985); Rai and Thiara (1997); Rose (1985).

13. It is interesting to note that even in 1985 when refuge conditions were, in general, much worse than today, Pahl (1985) found that 60 per cent of her respondents wanted to stay in a communal refuge.

14. Charles (1994); Delahay and Turner (1998).

Chapter 6

Moving Out, Moving On

A refuge is not just a safe place, a space where a woman can begin to recover from the effects of domestic violence. It is also a launching pad into a new phase of life. Work within the refuge is, from the outset, directed at supporting women to live independently, and moving from the refuge is an integral part of this whole process. It is not, however, an easy step to take. Women who have experienced the initial impact of leaving an abusive relationship (the *Reception* phase) and the emotional and practical challenges involved in the *Recognition* process, have now to leave a safe and supported environment, where they will have made friends and enjoyed the companionship of other women. In moving out, they must detach themselves, withdraw this emotional 'investment' from the refuge and reinvest it in the new community – making friends, joining local groups and taking part in local activities. This phase of *Reinvestment* is a time of further change, the construction of a new way of life and of dealing with all the challenges presented by independent living.

Of the six former residents who talked to me, only one had been able to return to her own home with appropriate safeguards. One had moved to supported accommodation for single women and four had been rehoused by the local authority or housing association. Of the current residents, four were not yet in a position to think about being rehoused, either because they had been in the refuge for a comparatively short space of time, or because of particular rehousing needs, but the remainder (13 in all) were expecting to move into independent accommodation and four were being rehoused in the next few weeks. These women and the former residents talked to me about their fears and hopes regarding their new lives, the problems they were experiencing in being rehoused and their need for support, both during the transitional period and in the longer term. For some of them, a radical shift in their perception of themselves and their approach to life had taken place and this change, which I refer to in Chapter 1 as *Realignment*, had had a profound effect on them and their relationships with others.

Problems of rehousing

Refuges have never been intended as long-term accommodation. In the late 1970s, it was thought that a period of about three months would be sufficient to enable a woman to recover, think about her future options and make decisions.[1] Writing in 2001, Levison and Harwin suggested that a normal stay should be between three and six months, since beyond that time women would want more privacy and independence and a settled way of life for themselves and their children, rather than the inevitable crises of refuge life. My interviewees confirmed this, saying that beyond this time, the limitations and restrictions of the accommodation became more obvious and irksome. As Barbara said: 'You begin to notice the cracks!' Moving out, however, depended on being able to return, in safety, to their former homes, or more likely on being rehoused.

Limited financial resources mean that women are more likely to be dependent on local authority housing or registered social landlords such as housing associations, which are playing an increasingly important role in the provision of social housing in many areas. The shortage of these types of housing stock is a major problem in many areas of the country, including those in this study, creating long delays and inevitable pressures on service providers and applicants. The evidence from this study and from other research suggests that although there have been improvements, women experiencing domestic violence still tend to be made offers of less popular housing in less attractive areas and in poor condition, the inference being that they are considered less deserving.[2] This was certainly the perception of the women, who felt that they were given less consideration when it came to rehousing, as well as in other areas of social need. Amalie was blunt – and bitter: 'For all intents and purposes, we're classed as second-class citizens now. We're not actually people – we're just statistics, really.' Workers agreed with this assessment, indicating that women could be offered properties that were inappropriate for them, or unsuitable for their needs. Examples quoted to me included offering third-floor maisonettes to women with very young children, flats with stairs only access for women with limited mobility and isolated housing with poor access to public transport, schools and communal facilities to young families. Asian women faced particular difficulties in moving on since, although they had a strong desire to maintain cultural links, there was a danger of being located by their families if they moved near to another Asian community. Living in an area where they were not known, however, could lead to isolation and might also be dangerous if they were subject to harassment.[3]

In her work as a refuge housing officer, Oriel was well aware of the frustration and despair which could be induced by the rehousing process:

> They get offered a lot of properties that are in no fit state. They've got a door and they have got a window and that's about it. A lot of women feel

very desperate when they're here and they'll end up taking properties that they wouldn't take if they weren't in that situation, that they wouldn't even consider. The housing situation is very precarious for women in refuges. Very, very hit and miss. Sometimes people can get nice properties, but the majority of times the properties are, you know, not what I would want to live in and not what I would expect a woman and children... It can be demoralising for them, especially when they've left somewhere nice. And most of the women who come in here have left somewhere nice.

Workers were also concerned that because landlords wanted houses occupied as soon as possible, women were placed under considerable pressure to inspect and make an immediate decision on a property. An additional source of pressure was the lack of the sort of intimate local knowledge to be aware of potentially danger-ous areas for themselves and their children. Maryam, a black resident, spoke of the fears that this generated:

I don't know none of the roads round here, I don't know none of the roads in none of the areas. So I could walk down a road and it's the wrong road, wrong turning. At the wrong time. Them things I think about. I think about my son. I don't want to be in that area where he might be associated with violence or associated with drugs or associated with any form of this nastiness. I don't want it for him. So, being in an area where I don't know, that just leaves me kind of crippled. Leaves my hands tied.

The offer of temporary accommodation was also a possibility in some areas and while this offered a way out of the refuge, women felt that the knowledge that they might have to move on again would result in feelings of insecurity, further disruption for children and a lack of incentives to integrate into a community.

The inability to find suitable accommodation of a reasonable quality within a realistic timescale has been identified for over two decades as the single most sig-nificant obstacle faced by women trying to leave an abusive relationship.[4] Not only may it stop them leaving, it may also force them to return. Women in all of the refuges gave me anecdotal evidence of other residents who had given up in despair of ever being rehoused and had returned to their partners. Long stays in the refuge mean that accommodation intended primarily for families in crisis is 'blocked'[5] and for some women this can lead to situations where families become institutionalised and over-dependent on refuge support. Excluding two women, whose exceptional circumstances had led to stays of 12 months, ten of the women in this study were currently or had been at the time of rehousing in a refuge for five months or longer. Val expressed the ambivalence of the long-stay residents, of wanting to go, but at the same time wanting to cling to the familiarity of the refuge that this induced:

I'm not ready to move anyway. I am and I'm not. I want to move because I want my own space and I want the kids to get settled, but I like the security of being here. Me friends are here and I feel safer here, so I don't want to move.

On the other hand, all of the workers were emphatic that it was possible to be rehoused too quickly, before a woman had been able to deal with the initial trauma of leaving the abusive situation, fully assess her options and make realistic choices which would enable her to live independently. One ex-resident, Maggie, had in fact come to the realisation that she had moved out from the refuge before she was ready and told me that, even with considerable support from workers, she was struggling emotionally and from a practical point of view to maintain the tenancy. The provision of accommodation close to but separate from the refuge (often referred to as 'second stage'), giving privacy and independence yet still within a supportive environment, might provide a solution to some of these problems, while easing the pressure on refuge accommodation. This type of accommodation is, however, in extremely short supply and was not available in the areas covered by this study.

Fears and hopes

However desperate women were to be rehoused, the offer of accommodation, when it came, provoked very mixed emotions. Women who had left or were about to leave described an initial sense of euphoria and excitement, but also apprehension as to what it would be like and concerns about their ability to make the transition to an independent life. Stacey caught this mixture perfectly: 'It's like leaving the nest, isn't it? You know, it's like Mum saying, "Well, go on, you can spread your wings and fly now".' As they talked about moving out, it became clear what a difficult transition women faced. Rehousing meant leaving the security of the refuge to live alone, or with just their children, most likely in a strange area and possibly in less than ideal conditions, taking total responsibility for their own lives, making decisions and managing their homes on their own. It was, as Leanne put it, 'scary'.

For all the women, safety was a major preoccupation. The fear of being found and of retribution was a constant in their lives. Even those who had changed their names felt that they would always be looking over their shoulders. They were very aware of the possibility of their former partners finding them and the physical and mental consequences for themselves and their children if this happened. Women wanted security in the form of extra door and window locks in their new homes, panic buttons and personal alarms for carrying with them. Without these many, like Eve, felt they would be paralysed by fear: 'I'll be locked in my house all the time. I daren't go out. And I don't want to feel like a prisoner in me own home.' These fears over personal safety and the continuation of violence are well founded, given the homicide figures quoted in Chapter 1. The 2004 British Crime Survey[6] also shows that, for a significant minority of women, physical and emotional abuse may continue for years after leaving, or change to a different form of abusive behaviour, such as stalking.

Women also talked of their concerns over more practical issues – furnishing, equipping and running their new home and providing for their family on a low income, how to create their own support network and the need to establish themselves in their new communities. With isolation from others having been a major feature in their experience of domestic violence, both residents and those who had already left spoke of their fears of being isolated and lonely after leaving the refuge.[7] Although their confidence and self-esteem had begun to improve over the time they had been in the refuge, women felt they still needed support from the refuge group if they were to tackle these issues and make a success of their new lives.

Two women who had previously been in other refuges and had left without ongoing support in fact told me that they had encountered so many problems that they had eventually gone back to their partners and later re-entered a refuge. The availability of ongoing support was, in their view, the factor that would have made the difference to them. The experience of those who had left had been that they had needed more intensive support during the time immediately before leaving and in the first three to six months afterwards. After this initial period, women felt more able to manage independently, although they welcomed some degree of continuing support after this time. It was also extremely important to them to know that they could still call on the support in the future.

In discussing how support was provided, there was a strong preference for a 'seamless' transition on leaving the refuge, with continuing support provided by someone they already knew and trusted, rather than having to build a new relationship.[8] Emotional support was seen as being as important as practical assistance and women particularly wanted to feel that they would be actively supported in their initial contacts with agencies and organisations.

Support after rehousing

Workers fully understood the problems that women faced in settling into a community; the strange and unfamiliar surroundings, the loneliness of being the only adult, the loss of friends and a safe environment. Oriel summed it up very simply: 'We take women so far, we support them so far in this safe environment here. But then they go out. And it's cold. And there's no one there.'

Women's Aid has always accepted that while some women will have gained sufficient strength, confidence and self-esteem during their time in the refuge to gain some control over their lives and go out and do it all themselves, the majority of women who leave the refuge are likely to need some form of continuing support for a period after they leave.[9] Limited resources have prevented this developing as rapidly as many groups would have liked and individual groups have adopted a wide variety of approaches to meet the needs of their service users. All three of the refuge groups provided telephone support to former residents and, at the time of this research, one of the groups was about to introduce a support service for women leaving the refuge, after assessing service needs and obtaining funding. The residents in this group were keen to know that the service would be in place before they left.

The other two groups were already operating support services for women who had left the refuge to move into independent accommodation and it is their services and the views of their service users that are referred to here. In one group, support was provided by the outreach and aftercare worker,[10] who took over the support role from the refuge workers once a tenancy had been proposed and if the woman had indicated that she wished to be supported. In the second group, women who wished to receive support in settling into their new homes were asked to name a volunteer or worker who they would like to work with them as a 'supporter'. If the suggested person was available and willing to be nominated, this arrangement was put in place. Women in this group were enthusiastic about the way this system operated; in particular the fact that they were able to work with someone they already knew that they could relate to, and the fact that they were in control of the process. Sophie said: 'It's like having a little friend outside and it's…I mean, I've got friends outside, but it's having that special person there what I can just phone up and say, Look, I need help.'

As their comments in the previous section show, the majority of women clearly wanted to be supported on leaving the refuge and the procedure in both groups was broadly similar. The worker or volunteer will discuss with the woman her needs and those of her family, and explain the scope and limitations of the scheme. A full risk assessment is carried out (and regularly updated) and a safety plan and procedures for both woman and worker agreed. Working together, they will draw up a formal support plan specifying their respective responsibilities, the amount of support that will be given and the aims and objectives it is hoped to work towards.[11] The woman will be supported in preparing to move, contacting utilities and other agencies, accessing grants and assembling furniture and essential equipment. Following the move, the support worker will work with the woman to help her settle into the new home, offering both practical and emotional support, using local knowledge to provide information and access to other types of support, so that the woman can develop her own network of contacts within the community. This support will be provided in regular visits, meetings, or telephone contact, according to the wishes of the woman.

In the first group, this support will initially be available for up to two months. For support beyond this timescale, there is access to the outreach service or to a regular weekly 'drop-in' session at the public office. In the second group this contact is for a longer period, initially for six months, extended to a year if mutually agreed. Workers said, however, that many women were happy to taper off and then terminate this support after a shorter period, in the knowledge that they could access further support via the outreach service at a later date. At the time of the study, this group also operated a weekly drop-in centre where residents and ex-residents, with their children, could meet for an informal lunch and some joint activities. The centre was set up to combat feelings of loneliness and isolation identified in a survey of previous residents. It was well used and enabled women to maintain links with former friends and workers if they so wished. It also gave children the opportunity to enjoy a play session with a children's worker and for women to ask for advice informally.

Both groups were very clear that the objective of providing support was to help the woman to bridge the gap between refuge life and the new community. As in the refuge environment, the aim is not to create dependency but to provide the practical and emotional support that will enable the woman to move forward, empower her to take control of her life and to make her own decisions. Penny explained:

> We're here to empower women and to ensure that, when they leave us, they've got a new life and they know all...we're not their only support system, you know, that they have developed an external support system. If they need support for the children, we make sure that they've got the family aid going in, the social worker that they know, the good relationship with the social worker, the education welfare officer they know, they know all the teachers, they know all the...you know, so that they've got that outside, they're empowered to go to the people. And they don't need to run back to us. We'll always be there, but...

And Tina emphasised the positive agency of the woman herself in creating this environment:

> We can't do it for her. We can only support her to do it. And give her the tools that can give her the information, the knowledge that she needs. But the rest of it, you know, you're just by her side.

Workers were aware that women might choose to return to their partners or, at a future date, form a new relationship. Such decisions, hopefully taken with fresh insight and understanding, would obviously affect issues around safety planning and risk assessment, but would rarely preclude the availability of support in some form or another. The sort of support described here was, of course, only available when women moved to accommodation within the area covered by the refuge services. Other women may move to refuges near where they hope to be rehoused and can utilise support services provided by that group. There are, however, areas of the country, particularly in rural areas, where this support is not readily available, although national helplines and internet access cover the whole of the UK. The provision of a network of fully funded and integrated support services was mentioned by many workers as a dream they would dearly love to see fulfilled.

Keeping in touch

The support of other women, which formed such a significant element in refuge life, remained important, but changed in its nature and scope once women had left the refuge. Jenny, about to be rehoused, commented that many promises were made and phone numbers exchanged when women initially left the refuge, but that contact rarely continued for more than a few months. Charlene, who had left the refuge some years previously, saw it as a gradual process of growing away from the first need to cling on to the familiar contacts, into independence and the growth of networks within the new community:

> We grew away. When I think about it, it was only because you support each other, don't you? And when you get out the refuge, you feel that's all there is. Just the girls that used to be...feel as though that's all there is out there, but there's not. There's not, there's all...you've got to go and find it. And you've got to make that move to find it, not somebody else do it for you. Yes, you got to do it.

Former residents said that as they had gained confidence they asserted their own values and boundaries and chose carefully who they wished to keep in touch with, but that the contacts they did maintain were highly valued and included social visits, outings and trips with their children.[12] In some refuges, ex-residents have got together to run their own support groups, but this had not yet occurred in the groups who worked with me. The growth in mobile phone usage, commented on in Chapter 3, facilitated these contacts, but also gave women the chance to maintain it at 'arm's length' if they so wished.

What was of particular importance to the women who had left the refuge and to those who would shortly be leaving, was the knowledge that there was still a community which would be there for them, centred on the refuge group. They felt totally confident that there would be emotional support and practical help for them if they needed it. This might be through the national or local helplines, by texting or phoning staff or women they were still in touch with, by visiting drop-in groups and centres, or using the outreach services. It was also important to them that this help would be available in the long term. Women needed to know that if problems related to their past experiences, such as legal proceedings or renewed contact from their abuser, resurfaced, or new instances of domestic violence occurred, they could readily access support. This was in complete contrast to the lack of knowledge and resultant inability to take action described in Chapter 2.

Ex-residents felt the knowledge that they could, if necessary, access support was the key factor that had enabled them to go out and build links with their new community. Even when they had needed a very limited amount of support, or none at all, it had provided valuable reassurance, at a time of extreme vulnerability, just to know that someone would be there if they needed help. This confidence stemmed not just from the fact that help would be available, but from the knowledge that there was a place, and people, where they didn't have to justify or explain themselves; where they would be believed and understood and where the need for vigilance and discretion, to ensure safety, could be relaxed for a while. Barbara said:

> It's nice to know that you can still just, sort of, drop in a chair or whatever and have a chat with somebody you know knows your circumstances. Because maybe you don't want to let other people know. Whereas here, you know, they know your circumstances.

This sense of belonging to a community which accepts you for who and what you are takes its place in Maslow's hierarchy of human needs (Figure 1.1, p.22) as one of the essential 'building blocks' in the growth of self-esteem and confidence. Women were uncertain if they would find a similar acceptance within their new communities. Having been in a refuge, however good the experience had been for them, was still felt by the majority of these women as imposing a stigma insofar as the public perception of them was concerned, and however many friends they made in their new community, this was an aspect that most of them preferred to keep hidden. There is still an immense lack of understanding of the effects of domestic violence within society. Talking about my research in daily life or on social occasions has, in general, met with two responses – either a flat refusal to acknowledge the topic, or a subsequent surreptitious discussion with women who had escaped domestic violence, or were still experiencing it. These women all saw the abuse as a matter to be kept hidden because they feared condemnation or retribution from their abusers, but they wanted very much to share their experience with someone who could understand and was not likely to judge them.

Beginning a new life

There was a very positive attitude among former residents and, despite their fears, among most of those who were hoping to be rehoused in the very near future; a sense of excitement that the world was beginning to open up for them, even if it wasn't going to be easy:

> I've walked away with nothing. I'm 38 and I'm having to start all over again. And it's been hard, you know, but it'll be worth it in the end. Because I know, if I go out and buy some nice glasses, I'm not going to have them thrown at me. I'm not going to have a coffee table thrown through the window because he's in a bad mood. No. (Stacey)

> I want to do so much, because I've never been allowed to, but it's hard, plucking up courage and doing it. And…and I know I'll be good at it, I know I will, because I've always wanted to do things, but it's just hard, the thought of being in the big, bad world again! (Liz)

Among those who were about to leave or had already been rehoused there was also a general appreciation of what they had gained from their stay in the refuge, coupled with a sense of wanting to give something back, or helping other women in some way, but this was still vague and ill defined, at this stage, for most of them. Three ex-residents were already doing voluntary work which supported women and children, one in the refuge where she had been a resident some years before. Others were intending to look for some type of work on leaving, but were concerned that, given the trauma their children had gone through, it might be more important to be at home for a while, to provide stability and reassurance. A further consideration was the fact that the wages they could earn would not cover the costs of childcare, work expenses, or the loss of direct and associated benefits. They were also worried about possible adverse reactions of potential employers to them – something that Liz felt she had experienced in her search for voluntary work mentioned in Chapter 4. Several felt that resuming their education was the key to a better future, but were uncertain as to what to go for. Even this uncertainty could be exciting – as Amalie said: 'I've got a lifetime ahead of me to find out what I want!'

On a more practical level, women still in the refuge were looking forward to furnishing their own places, pulling together furniture and possessions from whatever sources were available, or retrieving their possessions from storage and creating their own setting. This was something that former residents had found very pleasing and extremely satisfying. Charmian had completely redecorated her new home, an achievement that had given her particular satisfaction since her previous partner had told her she was hopeless and 'couldn't put brush to paint'. In the process, she had politely but firmly refused assistance from other family members, asserting her independence and the need to make her own decisions, establishing her boundaries and putting her own needs first.[13]

Realignment

This drive to develop their own abilities, establish their own way of life, reach out to life, but also to set boundaries for themselves and others, was evident in all the women who were expecting to be rehoused in the near future and in all but one of the former residents. The sole exception was Maggie (mentioned earlier in this chapter) who felt that she had left the refuge before she had really been ready to take this step. Underlying their words and actions was a clear and positive perception of themselves, their own identity and their role in society. These nine women had thought long and hard about their experiences and those of other women during their time in the refuge and this, as they told me, had resulted in a changed perception of who they were, what they stood for in terms of rights and responsibilities and the need to express their new values in their behaviour:

> It's made me a stronger person. Being aware of what I want, instead of just getting on with stuff that I don't really want to do. I'm able to say, no, I don't want to do that, you know. And you should be able to say that. Your own identity…you find it by just being yourself. (Charlene)

As with Charmian and her decorating, this change extended to family and friends, but also, perhaps more crucially, to insisting on respect and a sense of personal dignity in new relationships:

> I won't ever go there again. I will not be yelled at like I'm…you know, like I'm just nothing to anybody. That I will not be yelled and screamed at like a piece of rubbish. I just won't take it. (Jenny)

Once established, this did not appear to be a shifting dimension, but a radical and permanent change. This did not mean, however, that women who were aware of this change in themselves had 'come through' the process of recovery and had no need of further support. In some ways, it added to their challenges, since they were all still dealing with the practical and emotional problems of their situation. Now, they had also to examine the implications of their new understanding for themselves, their families and friends, who had known them differently and for the future. As Liz explained, this process of questioning and challenging her ideas and behaviours was extremely difficult, but worth doing: 'It's not easy and it's a long hard road to go by. But through everything I've been through and everything I've took, I got something worthwhile.'

A further perspective on this shift in attitude came from workers in specialist Asian refuges,[14] who pointed out that with their service users this was often a much longer and more difficult process. Due to the control which had previously been exercised over them by their families, these women were deeply involved, both while they were in the refuge and afterwards, in the search to find out who they were in the first place and establish themselves as people with their own identities.

What were the factors that had led to these changed views, which seemed to be a key element in the successful transition to independent living? What separated these women from the other residents who did not appear, at that time, to have adopted this different perspective? In Chapter 1, I used the term *Realignment* to describe this shift in understanding and identified it as fulfilling Maslow's concept of self-actualisation – the development of one's own ideals and abilities, the reaching out to achieve what one is capable of. Maslow suggests that a shift of this nature can only be contemplated once the basic necessities for survival (food, water, shelter) are secured and a sense of safety and the assurance of being accepted and belonging to a community begin to be internalised. These conditions encourage the growth of confidence and self-esteem which, in turn, enable human beings to reach out, take risks and explore new dimensions of themselves.

The one factor common to all of these women was their stay in the refuge, during which they were living with other women who had experienced domestic violence. It seems probable, then, that the provision of a physically and mentally safe environment, the approach to support adopted in the refuge and the shared experiences of residents had provided the infrastructure outlined by Maslow. This had enabled women to move beyond the continuum described in Chapter 3; from feeling they were worthless to a degree of confidence in themselves and their abilities, a sense of self and a realisation of what they were capable of. Other factors may have influenced this process; the personality of the woman herself, the availability of external support networks, or a combination of these and other factors. Seven of the nine women had been involved in counselling or group work, which may be a relevant factor or simply indicate that these women felt that counselling had something to offer them as individuals.

Workers in all the refuges commented that they were accustomed to this change in attitude taking place among the women they worked with, but that it was not invariable and might also take place once a woman had left the refuge and had had time and space to reflect on her experiences. Early research into the support work of Women's Aid refuges[15] showed that the provision of a safe environment and the opportunity to share experiences with other women who had experienced domestic violence had led women to the same changed perception of themselves and their roles in society, together with an understanding that they did not need to feel guilty or blame themselves for the violence. Similar claims in more recent research have been made for self-help and support groups for women in a complex range of situations,[16] indicating the way in which women can offer each other support, strength and self-understanding.

Although a comparatively small number of women were involved in this aspect of the research project, their views add further evidence to these claims and how this process of support works; by establishing, in line with Maslow's ideas, a safe and supportive community in which a woman can re-establish her connections to others and rebuild the confidence damaged by domestic violence. It also emphasises the importance of the knowledge that this support remains available in the long term, empowering women to move forward in their lives.

Summary

- Support in the refuge aims to empower women to live independently. Moving out, a process I have termed *Reinvestment* in Chapter 1, presents both challenges and opportunities for personal growth.

- Finding suitable accommodation of a reasonable quality within a realistic timescale remains the single most significant obstacle which women faced in leaving abusive relationships.

- Despite improvements in policy and practice, women tended to be offered less popular housing, often in poor condition and unsuited to their needs. They were often placed under pressure to inspect and make an immediate decision on a property. Asian women faced particular difficulties in finding appropriate accommodation.

- Long stays in refuges block beds for families in crisis and may lead to women becoming institutionalised and over-dependent on refuge support. Being rehoused too quickly, however, may mean that a woman is still in a state of shock and not fully able to deal with the pressures of living independently.

- Temporary accommodation was likely to result in a further move, often at short notice, causing disruption to education and a lack of incentives to become part of a community.

- Personal safety was a prime consideration for women who remained fearful of the consequences of being found and requested additional security fittings in their new homes, including personal alarms and panic buttons.

- Major concerns on being rehoused were isolation and loneliness, lack of support and the difficulties of establishing and maintaining the home on a low income.

- Women wanted support immediately before leaving the refuge and during the first three to six months following, preferring to receive this from a worker that they already knew and trusted. It was also important to know that they could continue to access support in the longer term.

- For women who were rehoused in areas where no outreach or support services are available, national helplines and websites can offer some assistance. The provision of a network of fully funded and integrated support services was mentioned by many workers as a dream that they would like to see fulfilled.

- Risk assessment and safety planning for both women and workers was an essential aspect of support work and needed to be regularly updated.

- Key elements in successful support giving were a jointly prepared support plan, clear aims and objectives and regular contact. Both practical and emotional support were necessary in helping women to bridge the gap between the refuge life and the new community.

- Because of low levels of confidence and self-esteem, women preferred the active involvement of workers in making new contacts.

- Women gradually developed new support networks, but maintained close links with a small number of the women they had met during their time in the refuge. They drew strength from the knowledge that they were understood and accepted by these women and by the refuge network, but were doubtful of the reactions of their new communities to any disclosures.

- Among the majority of former residents and those about to be rehoused there was a very positive attitude towards their new lives and a determination to 'make it work'. These women had developed a clear sense of their own identity, their rights as individuals and their role in society which I have described as *Realignment*. The reasons for this change were complex, but appeared to be directly related to their experiences in the refuge.

Notes

1. McGibbon, Cooper and Kelly (1989).
2. Barron (2002); Batsleer *et al.* (2002); Charles (1994); Davis (2003); Morley (2000).
3. Personal communications from specialist Asian workers from workshops held at the conferences of the Women's Aid Federation of England. Similar findings come from Batsleer *et al.* (2002) and Davis (2003).
4. Binney *et al.* (1981); Charles (1994); Dobash and Dobash (1992); Kirkwood (1993); Malos and Hague (1993); Mama (1996).
5. Ball (1994); Charles (1994).
6. Walby and Allen (2004). The survey also confirms earlier findings by Hester and Pearson (1998) that arrangements for child contact can be occasions for further abuse to take place.

7. Humphreys and Thiara (2002) found that financial hardship, lack of support, isolation and fears over personal safety were the problems most frequently reported by women who were living independently, with the most vulnerable period being the first six months after leaving the refuge. These issues continued to be a major problem for a longer period in the case of women from minority ethnic communities.

8. The importance of building trust in the support worker and of establishing a long-term relationship in promoting successful outcomes was also noted by Ball (1994) and Parmar, Sampson and Diamond (2005).

9. There is a considerable body of research confirming women's need for some degree of continuing support both once they have returned to life in a community and in the longer term, and the value of this support in helping families to build new lives and sustain tenancies (Batsleer *et al.* 2002; Charles 1994; Humphries and Thiara 2002; Lodge *et al.* 2001; McGee 2000a; Rai and Thiara 1997; Turner 1996). Similar evidence on the value of this support comes from a report prepared for Shelter (Jones, Pleace and Quilgars 2002) on a rehousing project for previously homeless people, most of whom had experienced domestic violence.

10. The term *outreach* is used to describe support work with women and children who are not in a refuge and is also used in some groups to describe support in moving from the refuge into a community, although this is more often referred to as *resettlement*, or *aftercare*. The two services may be run by the same team or individual and may overlap to some extent. Increasingly, the term *floating support* is being used to describe both types of service.

11. Hester and Westmarland (2005) have identified the importance of establishing clear aims and objectives in successful support work and that outcomes were improved where women were supported in their initial contact with agencies.

12. Pahl (1985) found that more than three-quarters of her interviewees continued to maintain some contact with a number of former fellow residents after leaving the refuge.

13. The need to address, explore and meet one's own needs and establish the self in relationships with others have similarly been identified by Kirkwood (1993) as important dimensions in mapping the process of recovery. She also suggests a desire to work in some way to help other women, which was evident but still nascent in the majority of my interviewees.

14. These comments come from the workshops referred to in note 3.

15. Clifton (1985); Rose (1985).

16. Batsleer *et al.* (2002); Butler and Wintram (1991); Hester with Scott (2000); Mullender and Ward (1991).

Chapter 7

The Best Things Were...

Life in the refuge is a constantly changing process, fluid and dynamic, essentially chaotic and often messy. Because of the way in which different types of support are interlinked and embedded within the refuge environment, it is not always easy to identify which of them are the most significant, or what are the key elements that contribute most effectively to a woman's journey of recovery from domestic violence. When I asked women to tell me what, in their view, had been the most influential factors, both during their stay in the refuge and in moving on, there was a remarkable similarity in their accounts and in what they saw as having been really important to them. All of these topics had been mentioned earlier in our discussions, along with many other aspects of support, but were now being brought out and identified as having been of particular worth in helping women to recover from their experiences and rebuild their lives.

Safety, both on a physical and on a mental level, was the first and most crucial factor, both during the refuge stay and as women thought about moving out into a new community and the challenges that lay ahead. The remaining five factors – being treated with respect, a non-judgemental attitude, being believed, mutual help and support and time to talk and be heard – were all rated as being equal to each other and remained of equal value to them throughout the time in the refuge and in the way they looked to be treated as individuals in the future. Underlying all of these factors was the attitude and approach of the support workers and volunteers, which influenced and sustained the support given to women. This chapter brings together and discusses in more detail these factors and why they were seen by the women as so important in rebuilding the capacity to cope, once they moved back into the wider community.

Safety

For all of the women, the physical safety of the refuge was the foundation stone on which everything else rested. Many, like Liz, confessed: 'This is the first time in my life I've actually felt safe.' Domestic violence, whatever its nature (physical, sexual, emotional or in any other manifestation) removes, by its unpredictability, any sense of there being a 'safe place' to be, while they are in the relationship. In consequence, the refuge represented a sanctuary from the violence. Leanne said: 'It's the safety thing. It really is safe here. I think that you know that nobody can come and hurt you in the refuge.' As Chapter 2 showed, this feeling of physical safety was particularly important when women first arrived at the refuge, when they were still very much afraid of being followed and of retribution and were also uncertain as to what dangers might exist within this new and strange environment. As they settled in, these fears lessened, but women remained acutely aware of the need for physical safety. If the behaviour of another resident was seen as endangering this safety for the majority, these circumstances provoked one of the rare occasions when they felt justified in taking matters to the workers and asking them to take action.

Safety, for both women and workers, rested on the core principle that the security of the refuge must not be compromised and this required careful consideration of every aspect of the refuge routine, since even the smallest and most inadvertent action could endanger security. Post for residents and workers went to a box number, a fact which was often a cause for complaint by residents because of the delays it could cause in getting information to them. However, they understood that putting post through the door or giving the address in full would be an additional threat to security. Workers were careful to screen incoming telephone calls for or about residents to protect them from being traced and visitors such as workmen were carefully vetted and monitored. Refuge administrators tended to build up a list of people who they felt confident would understand and observe their precautions. Serious breaches of confidentiality or security by women themselves, or which resulted from the actions of others, were seen as endangering the lives of everyone who lived in, worked for, or visited the refuge and as a general rule meant that a woman would have to move on.[1] Workers also needed to protect their own security and personal information in order to avoid potential problems. As Daphne pointed out: 'Domestic violence is a very dangerous area to work in. This is not taking little old ladies for a walk along the prom.'

As the preceding chapter indicated, the need for physical safety remained a major concern for women who were preparing to leave the refuge and for those who had already moved out into a new community. Safety planning, safety procedures and ongoing risk assessment for the woman, her family and for support workers were vital components of support plans and an awareness of a continued need for confidentiality and security was seen as essential for all those agencies who might be involved with the family. For these women and their children safety will be, literally, a lifelong preoccupation.

Since this study was carried out, new threats to the physical safety of women escaping domestic violence have emerged in the development of satellite navigation, where exact positions can be tracked over the internet, and of mobile phone tracking systems, originally designed to enable parents to track their children and know that they were safe. Mobile phones which, as the accounts of women show, have become a source of help and support, can now become life threatening if they are used by abusers to stalk women and their children. There are simple steps that can be taken to safeguard their use and research is continuing into how women can remain safe while retaining the advantages which this technology offers them.[2]

Respect

The physical security of the refuge was, however, only one half of the safety equation. Even when they had begun to feel physically safe, women recognised that their feelings of emotional safety were still very precarious. The sort of 'mind games' described in Chapter 1 – constant criticism, ridicule and belittling, together with gradual isolation from other sources of support – had resulted in a state of constant fear, anxiety and doubt, so that a woman no longer trusted herself, or those around her. As a result, she had lost her sense of personal identity, self-worth and self-respect. Rachel saw regaining self-respect as the essential basis for rebuilding her life: 'I had to try and gain some respect for myself. I needed that and I think I got it. I think I got it. My self-respect was very, very damaged.'

To re-establish these feelings and restore a sense of emotional safety, personal integrity and a degree of trust in those around them was a much longer process than the establishment of physical safety, but women were very clear that consistently being treated with respect by those around them was the key element in this process. Workers saw themselves as committed to an attitude which respected the autonomy of women, so that they worked in partnership with them, supported them as they defined their problems, made choices and took their own actions, rather than imposing solutions.[3] This attitude of respect for service users also implied a respect for their privacy and personal space, a consideration which may have been all too absent in their previous lives. The desire not to be intrusive, however, had to be balanced against the need to ensure that a woman who might feel too nervous to ask for help, or who might feel intimidated by coming to a busy office, received the support she needed. Respect was also seen as entailing a two-way process in the requirement that women respected the terms of their tenancies, the house rules which provided the boundaries of the refuge environment and that they treated their fellow residents, workers and volunteers in the same way that they wanted to be treated.

Residents felt that respect for them included workers being 'upfront' with them; being open and honest about whatever was happening and giving clear information and explanations, so that they could make their own choices, even when this involved facing difficult choices and unpalatable facts. Being treated with respect and as individuals worthy of respect in this way was initially quite a difficult concept to take on board, since it was not an attitude which they had been accustomed to in the past, either from their abuser or, for many of them, from the agencies and organisations they had approached for help. It could also be difficult at first to grasp the concept of respect as involving a non-directive, self-help approach and see its value to them. Barbara said that she had puzzled over it:

> I mean, first of all, I couldn't understand why we had to keep trolling over to the other side of town to get forms done and that and I thought well, probably a simple phone call from the office… But it does make us go out and do these sort of things and I think that that's probably quite important, so I can see the reasons for that. And, again, then we're kind of in control of what we're doing.

Once they could believe it was genuine, the majority of women commented that giving back control over their lives in this way had built up their confidence, self-esteem and self-respect. They felt that they were being recognised as responsible members of society. A small number of women, however, had wanted a much more directive approach and felt that they had not received all the support they needed. As a result, they had felt angry and frustrated. Problems of this nature, which may have stemmed from a mismatch of expectations, did, however, seem comparatively rare.

The way in which self-respect, confidence and self-esteem had grown as a result of being treated with respect can be seen in the way women faced the challenges and fears of moving out into a new community. As Chapter 6 recounted, all except one of the women who had moved or were about to move out had experienced a major shift in their concepts of their place in society, which I have referred to as *Realignment*. An insistence on being treated with respect and as individuals with the right to take responsibility and make their own choices formed a major part of this attitude and extended to the agencies and organisations they needed to deal with, friends, family and particularly in new relationships.

A non-judgemental attitude, being believed

Accepting and believing a woman's experience of domestic violence can be seen simply as just another aspect of respect, as can the adoption of a non-judgemental approach. Both relate to the concept of respecting a woman as an autonomous individual who knows most about her own problems and has the inherent capability to solve them. Domestic violence, as the accounts in Chapter 1 indicated, creates conflicting pressures and difficult choices, within which a woman will take those actions which seem appropriate to her, but which are not always capable of being understood by others. Taking a non-judgemental attitude and believing her account conveys feelings of acceptance and empathy, which in themselves indicate respect for the individual and places her reality at the centre of support provision, rather than the judgements of those outside the situation. I have chosen, however, to separate these two factors from that of respect since, in talking to me, women themselves separated them out and laid particular emphasis on the value that these two factors had in helping them to move forward in their lives. As their stories showed, their experiences of domestic violence included constant adverse judgements on everything they did, of being followed or interrogated about every minute detail of their activities and being told that no one would ever believe them, or that it would all be seen as their fault. To be believed, trusted and free from destructive criticism and judgement was, therefore, immensely important to them. It further contributed to rebuilding confidence and self-esteem and worked to lessen their fears about the people around them. This, in turn, helped in the development of feelings of trust and emotional safety. It is no accident that believing (and, by implication, not judging) has been placed at the head of its declaration of values by Women's Aid.

An interesting sidelight on this issue was the anger expressed by several residents and former residents against those who they saw as abusing this approach, either, as Charmian described it, 'using the refuge to doss in', or, as others put it, 'using the system' and the support provided by the refuge and resettlement workers to unfairly obtain benefits such as accommodation, when they themselves were being honest and accurate about their problems and needs. Harriet was blunt about this:

> Because I did appreciate what the women [workers] do, I did *not* appreciate seeing other women taking the piss. I did not appreciate that at all, when you saw women taking advantage of the situation.

Workers pointed out that, because of the confidentiality they maintained about the affairs of women in the refuge, other residents might well be unaware of the full circumstances of a situation and perhaps have been making false assumptions.[4] Nevertheless, workers were aware that there were some instances where women may have been taking advantage of the refuge system to gain advantage in some way. However, as they pointed out, their whole approach is based on believing women's experiences and mutual honesty and trust, an approach which most of those who come to them for help understand and do not abuse.

Mutual help and support from other residents

Peer support has been an accepted and valued part of life in Women's Aid refuges since their inception, based on the belief of the Women's Liberation Movement that women can draw strength and hope from each other.[5] As the accounts of the women in this study show, this has remained the case. They consistently talked of the importance of this support in helping them to recover from domestic violence and the way in which both the giving and the receiving of support provided opportunities for personal understanding and development and the growth of self-esteem.

Although the flow of support was evident throughout the stay in the refuge, it gradually changed in nature as women moved from the acute distress and anxiety of the *Reception* phase into the more complex process of *Recognition*. On arrival, support was initially valued as showing women that they were not, as they had thought, alone in their experiences, as other women shared their stories, drew on their own insights to provide emotional support during this very difficult period and offered practical help and information about the requirements of the new life. Later on, this support became more reciprocal, building the self-esteem of those who had once been new arrivals by enabling them, in their turn, to give to others. Women shared shopping trips or leisure time and supported each other during times of emotional or practical stress. As Val put it to me: 'We are there for each other.' For some women, this experience of sharing with other women had eventually led to a deeper understanding of themselves and a changed perception of their rights as individuals (the concept of *Realignment* discussed in the preceding chapter).

Both residents and ex-residents were totally realistic about the pressures and frustrations caused by communal living and the difficulties that engaging with others could bring. They were, however, emphatic about the overall advantages they gained, both from the experience of living together, including learning to handle tensions and problems, and from the support they gained from other residents. This was particularly noticeable when they talked about how to improve refuge accommodation. Although there was a strong desire to improve personal privacy, both for mothers and for their children, their ideas (discussed in detail in Chapter 5) were centred on a communal form of living and facilities, such as shared space for cooking and eating which encouraged mutual support, while removing some of the more contentious aspects of sharing, such as having individual bathrooms and toilets. They all commented that in completely self-contained accommodation peer support could be more difficult to give and receive, unless special consideration was given to facilitating this process.

The refuge, then, despite its tensions and conflicts, provided women with a community where they could feel accepted and believed, express their feelings, deal with their experiences and support each other. Further evidence of the importance of the need to recognise that there was a community which was 'there for you' comes from the discussions with former residents. Although they were not, in general, likely to maintain contact with a large number of the women they had met in the refuge, the contacts they did maintain were very important to them and the fact that the refuge itself was there and that there were people in it who accepted them as they were gave them a sense of inner security which enabled them to move forward. They might never need any further support – the knowledge of the existence of an understanding community was enough. Many of them felt that the acceptance, understanding and support were unlikely to be as readily available in their new communities.

Time to talk and be heard

Discouraging women from talking to their family, friends or neighbours, or indeed chatting in the shops that they were allowed to use, had been a major part of their experience of domestic violence. As a consequence, women had become isolated from any form of communication other than that provided by their abuser, which was invariably negative in its content and effect. Several of them talked of needing to relearn their social skills in some respect or another. Stacey had to brace herself to be able to make telephone calls:

> Because I was never allowed to use the telephone when I lived with my ex-partner. I wasn't allowed to use it. I wasn't allowed to answer it and he pulled [the cord out]. I still don't like talking on the phone. I hate using the phone. It makes me quite nervous.

When they first came to the refuge, then, being able to talk freely again was immensely important to them – 'talking late into the night' so common in accounts of early refuge life, remained a constant theme in all the refuges, particularly so in the communal houses.

Women appeared to identify three strands of talking, all of which were of value to them. The first comprised the commonplaces of everyday conversation – about television, shopping, local activities and events – and might be exchanged with fellow residents, workers or other visitors to the refuge. This linked women back to the world beyond the refuge to which they would eventually be returning and helped to rebuild the social skills that might have become eroded as a result of domestic violence. The second strand was that of supportive talk – discussing past experience, offering emotional support, exchanging advice, information and ideas and planning for the future. Much of this came from other residents in the form of mutual support, but this was not always enough on its own. Conflict within the refuge, or the mix of residents, might make mutual support difficult, or women could feel 'stuck' with fellow residents who were at a different position in dealing with their problems.

Additionally, other residents might have pressing problems of their own which resulted in them not being available. Because of these possible difficulties, and because of their knowledge and experience, time to talk, both formally and informally, to workers and be heard by them, once feelings of emotional safety and trust had developed, was also a prime requirement. To some extent, this extension of the worker's role, in actively listening to women on an informal basis, as well as in their formal role of support worker, can also be seen as a further indication of respect, in that it shows that they are seen as worthy of being listened to. In general, women felt that this support was freely available to them, particularly on entry to the refuge. The importance that women attached to this factor was clearly indicated, however, by the feelings of resentment and, on occasions, real anger, when this support was temporarily not available to them because of pressure of work, staff shortages, hours of attendance, or other problems.

The third strand might be termed the 'healing talk' provided by group work, counselling or other professional contacts. Those who provided these services needed to be seen as sharing the values and concepts of refuge workers, but as standing aside from the day-to-day management of the refuge and being there to provide a space which was specially for them. Not all women felt a need for this third strand at the time that they talked to me, although a high proportion saw it as an important element in their search for personal understanding and development. The remainder felt that it could be of value in helping women and needed to be easily available for women who wanted to access it, both during the time in the refuge and afterwards. It was notable that all of the former residents who spoke to me had chosen to continue counselling, or take up some form of group work, after they had left the refuge and had found it had been a significant source of support.

Providing this opportunity to talk at all these levels would seem to be a necessary part of helping women to express their feelings, mourn their losses and restore a sense of normality to their lives.[6] It was also apparent from conversations with former residents that they still needed to maintain communicative links (but not necessarily gain active support) with a nucleus of people who understood where they were coming from, perhaps through contact with former refuge residents, use of outreach or aftercare support, or by using the drop-in centre, as well as networking within their new communities.

Giving the gift of time and understanding to individuals can, in itself, be a validating and supportive process; a point that was brought home to me by listening to the comments and reading the feedback which followed my interviews with women. They thanked me for listening to them and welcomed both the opportunity to talk, and the realisation that their ideas and views were considered to be worth listening to and might be used to help others. Workers had previously told me that women often developed new skills and built up confidence, but failed to realise this until an event or comment drew it to their attention. Our discussions seemed to have functioned in this way, enabling them to realise just how far they had come in their journey of recovery and this had provided an important marker for them. Janet said: 'The interview made me decide to be positive and to think of myself and what I want to do in the future.'

Attitude and approach of the workers

The factors that women identified as being of prime importance to them in reconstructing their lives depended, to a large extent, on the attitude and approach adopted by the workers both within the refuge and in supporting women into the wider community. Women defined this approach in very different ways, but it was something they were very aware of, appreciated and identified as being 'different' from the support offered by the other agencies that they had come in contact with. Whereas the roles of counsellors, children's workers and other specialist workers can be fairly well defined and their importance understood, that of the generalist worker, both in the refuge and in resettlement work, is far more diffused and embedded in the work of the refuge as a whole. It is only when all the facets of this work are brought together that the complex and demanding nature of the job and its importance to women can be appreciated.

Refuge workers are constantly dealing with women in crisis, most apparent when women first arrive at the refuge. At this time a high level of practical and emotional support is necessary. Later on in the process of recovery, workers need to constantly reassess the support needed by each woman, trying to maintain a delicate balance between support and challenge, independence and dependency, encouragement and advocacy, while ensuring that the women receive the level of support that they need and respecting their privacy and personal space. This difficult task is made more complex by the variety of emotional and practical problems experienced by residents and their expectations of workers. The ultimate goal of the work is to empower the woman to take control of her own life and support her back into the community, able to live independently and with confidence in her own ability to handle the situations she will meet. At the same time as providing these differing levels of support, workers need to facilitate the communal life of the refuge, acting to reduce tensions and to encourage the support which women can give to each other. It is not easy to balance all these factors and hardly surprising that, from time to time, there is a failure in communication and support needs are not met.

What was it that women identified as 'different' in the approach which lay behind this work, and what did it mean to them? Many of their comments have been drawn out in earlier chapters – women felt believed and treated with respect and that workers took time out to listen to them. Workers were consistent in their approach, set clear boundaries and were tough where it was necessary. Underlying these themes, women sensed that there was a genuine care for them as individuals. Rachel described it as 'love, really, love'. Harriet and Stacey, in refuges far distant from one another, made identical comments: 'They've been there all the way for me.' Marti wrote me a letter to explain what she was unable to say aloud: 'I cry as I write this. No one in my family wants me, but total strangers do.'

Workers themselves identified their approach as placing women's needs and perspectives at the centre of the support they provided and that this commitment was the motivation for their work. Daphne put it very simply: 'I am here for the women, the kids.' Jay was very clear about what made the difference:

> Putting women and children central to your service. So that you look…everything that happens, you're looking at how that affects that woman and that child. And within that, it's around respect for service users. And I think that's what you don't get elsewhere all the time. And making sure that, whatever you do, your driving force behind it is to secure the safety of women and children experiencing domestic violence. I think that's…that's the important thing. And I *believe* in women for women's services. I *believe* in empowerment. I don't believe in taking women's choices away from them.

To maintain this level of commitment, and the flexibility to work with so many differing needs, imposed considerable emotional strains. Workers spoke of the 'relentless pressure' of refuge life and the stressful and draining nature of their work. Additional pressures were caused by the constantly changing environment in which refuges now operate. Changes in legislation, policy and regulatory measures require high levels of professional skills and knowledge that need to be constantly updated, and funders have detailed requirements for monitoring and evaluation. Additionally, the growth of interagency working, although a welcome development, requires attendance at numerous meetings, if the grassroots experience of the needs of women who experience domestic violence is to be carried forward into service provision. For those supporting women back into the community, time and effort needed to be invested in liaison with workers in other fields, in order that women can successfully make the transition to independent living. All these requirements had to be met, but there were rarely additional financial resources available for staffing. It was apparent that workers often met these demands by working outside their normal hours.[7] They expressed the opinion that the work they did in providing emotional and practical support was not understood or properly valued by funders. They were fearful that the growing volume of other work might mean they were not able to spend sufficient time on what they felt should be the main focus of their work – the needs of women who had experienced domestic violence.

Both generalist and specialist workers emphasised the need for them to have the sort of support that would enable them to discuss their problems, share experiences and 'download' the emotional pressures. On a day-to-day basis, this support was drawn both from those around them and from colleagues and line managers within the refuge group, many of whom had had experience of working in the refuge. This support was highly valued, as Sadie explained:

> Yeah, it is stressful and, you know, events that it throws up are stressful. That's why I think it's so important that we're not on our own. You know there's going to be one, two, three people that you can chat things over with and get opinions on and just…just have somebody listen to you and say 'oh, you dealt with that really well' or 'perhaps we could do this' or… For me, that's invaluable. There's not a member of staff in this team whose opinion I don't value. However good you are at dealing with a situation, somebody will always come up with a different angle on it, something you just hadn't thought of and it will make things a bit easier and things will fall into place a little bit more and…I think it's wonderful. Wonderful.

It was also important that the group shared a common sense of purpose, a focus for their work and a direction for the future, which enabled workers to see beyond the day-to-day demands of the situation.

Rebuilding the capacity to cope

In Chapter 1, women talked of the ways in which domestic violence had impacted on their lives; how the cumulative effects of physical and emotional abuse had removed any concept of physical or mental safety, isolated them from potential sources of support, reduced their ability to trust themselves or those around them and destroyed their sense of self-worth, confidence and self-respect. Even in these conditions, they spoke of the various ways in which they had struggled to protect and care for themselves and their children and minimise the impact of the abuse.

I suggested that their reactions to domestic violence and the decisions and actions that they took could more readily be understood by seeing them in terms of Maslow's hierarchy of human needs, discussed in Chapter 1 and shown in diagrammatic form in Figure 1.1 (p.22). For these women, the uncertainty and unpredictability of domestic violence had taken away the base requirements of safety, security and freedom from fear, severed connections to others and damaged self-esteem. All that remained was the basic need to sustain life – for food, water and shelter. For some, life itself was at risk if the relationship continued. Yet, in line with Maslow's ideas, women were positively and actively taking action to meet their own needs as far as they were able, even though they were severely restricted in what they were able to achieve.

In this chapter, I have focused on the factors that women said were especially important to them and which, although present in earlier chapters, were interwoven with other strands of support. In bringing them together and looking at them in more detail, it is clear that they are the essential 'building blocks' of Maslow's structure and that they work together to help women in the task of regaining full autonomy and control over their own lives. This process started with the base line of the physical safety and security of the refuge, within which women discovered that they were not alone in their experiences, but that there were other women in the same situation, giving them a community to connect to and a sense of belonging. The attitude of belief and a non-judgemental approach adopted by workers started the regeneration of self-esteem and also contributed to the stability of mental safety and freedom from fear. Finally, the overarching principles of empowerment and respect for the individual as a responsible and capable member of society fostered the growth of confidence, a sense of personal worth and self-esteem. Morris, whose work on emotional literacy is well known, noticed that these same factors were those that influenced the growth of self-esteem in the people she worked with:

> I was very struck by how self-esteem seemed to evolve in response to being treated with respect, empathy and genuineness and how it flowered in environments where the individual was physically and emotionally safe, had clearly defined boundaries which were consistently held and took an active part in any decision making. (Morris 2001, p.16)

This rebuilding process is neither straightforward, nor simple. As women have described, it can be extremely difficult to relearn ways of living and confidence and self-esteem can be easily knocked back by events that others might regard as trivial. Nevertheless, working in this way, to rebuild the capability to cope, is essential if a woman is to come to terms with the losses she has sustained, both through the relationship and in leaving it, adjust to the changes that have become necessary and move forward in her life.

Summary

- Support systems within the refuge are interlinked and embedded in their environment. Women identified six factors within these systems which they saw as having been of particular worth in helping them to recover from their experiences and rebuild their lives.

- Physical and mental safety were placed first. The other factors, seen as equal to each other in value, were being treated with respect, an approach which believed and did not judge them, mutual support and time to talk and be heard. All these factors were influenced and sustained by the attitude and approach of the workers.

- Physical safety was the first essential on which all support rested, since domestic violence removes any sense of there being a 'safe place' to be. Ensuring that the security of the refuge and the current and former residents was not compromised required constant vigilance on the part of women, workers and all those who came in contact with the unit, or the women who lived there. This included any outside agencies.

- An additional threat to safety has been posed by recent developments in technology, which can enable women to be tracked by global positioning systems, or by mobile phones fitted with tracking devices. Precautionary measures need to be taken to neutralise this problem.

- Being treated with respect and as a capable and responsible member of society helped women to regain the self-respect and sense of personal worth which had been damaged by domestic violence.

- Respect on the part of workers involved working in partnership with women, supporting them to define their problems, make choices and take their own actions, rather than imposing solutions, or taking action on their behalf. It included being open and honest about situations and difficulties so that women could make fully informed decisions.

- This approach was different from any previously encountered and women initially found it hard to understand. The majority found that this approach had helped them to regain their self-respect and integrate this into their new lives. A small minority, however, had wanted a much more directive approach and felt that they had not received the support they needed.

- Taking a non-judgemental approach and believing women's accounts of their experiences counteracted the constant criticism and surveillance they had previously endured and further contributed to the growth of confidence and self-esteem. The vast majority of women understood and appreciated the trust that was placed in them and did not abuse it.

- Mutual help and support from other residents enabled women to understand that they were not alone in their experiences of domestic violence, to gain strength from others and offer support during times of emotional or practical need, providing a community where they were believed and accepted.

- Because of the isolation imposed on them by their abuser, time to talk and be heard was considered very important by women. It appeared to be needed on three levels – everyday conversation, which helped to restore social skills eroded by domestic violence, talk which was emotionally or practically supportive and the type of 'healing' talk provided by counselling or group work. Women valued the gift of time and understanding and actively sought to communicate on a variety of levels.

- All of these factors were seen as continuing to be important after leaving the refuge and women looked to be treated in this way by other agencies, their family and friends and, notably, in any other relationships they might develop.

- The approach and attitude of workers was crucial in maintaining the value of these factors. This was perceived by the women as showing a genuine care for them as individuals, which had nurtured their own self-respect and enabled them to move forward.

- The demands of refuge work and the levels of stress involved meant that workers needed to be able to talk over problems and be supported by colleagues and line managers and to feel that their work was valued.

- Domestic violence had demolished the structure of women's previous lives, leaving only the basic need for survival. All of the above factors worked together to rebuild this structure, in line with Maslow's ideas of human need and restore the capacity to handle the recovery from the losses which had been sustained during the relationship and in leaving.

Notes

1. This could include actions by outside agencies, as shown in Chapter 2, when an agency letter sent to a home address revealed a woman's location to her abuser.

2. Valuable research into this problem has been carried out at the University of Plymouth and a brief guide to the dangers and sensible precautions can be found in Atkinson (2005).

3. Valuing and respecting the individual and giving her back control over her choices and decisions have similarly been recognised as crucial in varied approaches to the concept of empowerment (Croft and Beresford 1989).

4. Batsleer *et al.* (2002) reported similar feelings among their interviewees and this raises interesting questions about women defining other women as 'worthy' or 'unworthy' without, perhaps, fully understanding the struggles that may be going on for them.

5. Mullender and Ward (1991).

6. These factors were also noted as being significant by Coleman and Guildford (2001).

7. A point also noted by Ball (1994).

Chapter 8

Putting the Pieces (Back) Together

Domestic violence and abuse exact a heavy cost from those who experience it, in terms of their physical and emotional well-being, social and economic deprivation and personal integrity. The consequences are also likely to be felt by family and friends and by a wider circle that may include employers, health services, school authorities and the statutory and voluntary agencies which may be called upon to take action or provide support. Nor is it simply a short-term problem, calling only for crisis intervention. Recovery from the effects of domestic violence is likely to be a long-term process, both in rebuilding the physical and practical framework of life and in restoring the confidence and emotional capability necessary for independent living. Translating this impact into financial terms, the overall costs of domestic violence in England and Wales, including the cost in human and emotional terms, have been estimated at a staggering £23 billion a year.[1] Understanding these broader issues is of major importance in terms of political activity and policy making. It can, however, be easy to forget that at the centre of any incident of domestic violence is an individual human being, usually a woman, and that listening to her voice is of equal importance in framing policy and informing practice.

The women who took part in this project talked candidly to me about their thoughts and feelings, the effect that domestic violence had had and was still having on them, the problems they had faced and were facing and the challenges involved in moving on. They discussed the benefits and drawbacks of refuge life, offered constructive thoughts on where improvements could be made and identified very clearly the type and style of support which had had a positive and effective influence on them. Further insights have come from the experience of refuge workers, managers and workers with specialised knowledge of housing, children's work and counselling. These direct and compelling voices described a rich and detailed picture of needs and responses, which at first sight seemed fluid, random and chaotic. As I listened to these accounts and observed the interactions which took place within the refuges, however, I realised that an underlying structure was emerging, which provided a way of understanding what was happening and the pathway from loss towards recovery that women appeared to be following. This journey took them from the realisation of the need to leave the relationship and their feelings of being and having nothing, to a developing confidence in their ability to live independently. Two interlinked concepts influenced this progression: a pattern of recovery from loss, and the effect that domestic violence had had on their personal sense of integrity and self-worth.

The theories behind these ideas (recovery from bereavement and Maslow's hierarchy of human needs) were detailed in Chapter 1. This concluding chapter brings together these theoretical perspectives and the realities of domestic violence and recovery as women experienced them. It will also discuss how this model can be used to inform effective support giving in a variety of settings and its application to other forms of domestic violence.

Loss, transition and recovery

Leaving an abusive relationship, whether or not this includes a stay in a refuge, will involve facing the prospect of loss. In material terms, women had lost their homes and most of their possessions, including the small, irreplaceable treasures such as family photos or children's drawings. Some had also had to give up jobs and all of them had lost personal financial security, a loss which was likely to significantly disadvantage them over a very long period of time. On an emotional level, women talked of the loss of the relationship, where conflicting feelings of love, fear, guilt and uncertainty coexisted, but they also mourned the severing of links to family and friends and, for some of them, the older children or pets that had had to be left behind. The overriding need to remain safe and the risks of making contact (both for themselves and those they loved) could mean that these links might never be renewed. In addition, there was the loss of a setting (home, neighbourhood, town) which, however difficult existence there had become, was still a place to which they were attached and which was known and understood. Almost half the women had made journeys of over 100 miles to reach a refuge; four had travelled more than 300 miles from everything they knew. Although women recognised and appreciated the fact that they were safe, their feelings of dislocation, even when much shorter distances were involved, added an extra dimension to their emotional losses.

In listening to the way the theme of loss ran through all their accounts and the impact that it had had on women, I saw a distinct similarity between their experiences and those which have been generally regarded as taking place over an extended period of time following bereavement; an intense initial reaction and a phase of acknowledgement and adjustment, followed by the transition to a new life. These phases, explored in more detail in Chapter 1, are acknowledged by researchers as being fluid and overlapping, with two separate sources of pressure existing within them; the differing practical tasks to be accomplished during each phase and the underlying emotional distress.

Looking at recovery from the impact of domestic violence in this way, the effort of leaving the relationship and arriving at the refuge can be seen as the point at which the initial impact is felt. In Chapter 2 women talked of their feelings at this time – shock, numbness, a sense of unreality and of their need for time and space to 'get their heads round' what had happened to them. I described this as the *Reception* phase. Over time, they moved to a transitional phase, which I have termed *Recognition*, where they were able to acknowledge the reality of the changed situation and begin to make adjustments. During this period, as they discussed in Chapter 3, the full extent of their material and emotional losses became apparent, their feelings of anger began to be expressed, in both direct and indirect ways, and they experienced intense and unpredictable waves of emotional distress. Finally, they needed to enter a phase of *Reinvestment*, facing the challenges involved in moving out, which they described in Chapter 6, establishing a new life for themselves and their families and 'investing' emotionally in a new community. As in bereavement, women moved forward and back between these phases. At each of them there were different practical tasks to be accomplished, and underlying all of them were the emotional tensions that had the capacity to pull them down, or provide the energy to propel them forward.

The extra burden

In the case of the death of a friend or family member, recovery from the practical and emotional stresses of bereavement can be made more difficult by the circumstances surrounding the death, or by the complex nature of the relationship with the person who has died. Murder, suicide or the losses of a child or sibling are among the many factors that can affect the pattern of recovery. For women who have experienced domestic violence, the additional burden that they carry, as they work through the process of recovery, is the effect that the abuse has had on them as autonomous individuals. This can also be seen as a further aspect of loss, but of losses which have built up, almost unnoticed, over the period of the relationship and which women described so vividly in Chapter 1: the loss of physical and mental safety; loss of social contact; of the power of independent thought; confidence and a sense of personal self-worth; and justifiable aspirations. Yet even within these constraints, women talked of the ways in which they did whatever was possible to satisfy their needs for communication and contact, bearing in mind that their prime concern was keeping themselves and their children as safe as possible from abuse and violence. This aspect of domestic violence is unlikely to be as obvious as the physical indications of abuse. As women said to me, they might look and sound 'all right' and be striving to maintain some semblance of normality for their children, but it was the mental abuse, with all its facets of control and manipulation, which they found most destructive of their individuality, creating a sense of utter unworthiness which was intensely hard to overcome. Not only did it make it more difficult to take the decision to leave the relationship permanently, but it had a major impact on their ability to work through the process of recovery from the emotional and material losses they had suffered and rebuild their lives.

Based on these detailed accounts of the effects of domestic violence, I suggested that they could be more easily understood by placing them within the context of Maslow's hierarchy of human needs (Figure 1.1, p.22), recognising that women were trying to meet their needs for safety and to reach out to others, but that they were held back by the difficulties of the abusive situation. Nurturing this capacity to take positive action and the restoration of personal autonomy were identified by the women as being key elements in their move towards independent living, although, as they commented, this was not an easy transition to make when their lives had been so rigidly controlled and they were used to being told what to do. Of particular importance in rebuilding these abilities, as they discussed in Chapter 7, was the community support available from the different sectors of the refuge environment – workers, volunteers and residents.

How these concepts affect support giving

Seeing the process of rebuilding lives in this way – as recovery from immense loss, made more complex and stressful by the effects of domestic violence – offers new insights into the support needs of women escaping abusive relationships. Support can be seen not as an unspecified and undifferentiated package, but as facilitating a structured process which will extend from the time a woman leaves the relationship until some time after she has been living independently. Within this process there will exist two separate but interlinked and equally necessary aspects of support – practical and emotional. Practical support – information, assistance and, at times, advocacy – will vary with each phase of recovery, from the initial tasks of settling in, registration and obtaining access to benefits, through the transitional phase where legal issues, housing and education may need to be considered, to the process of moving out and settling into a new community. Practical support is also concerned with the establishment of a physically safe and secure environment – first priority of every woman who took part in this research. Emotional support was an essential and complementary requirement throughout this process, enabling women to regain their sense of mental safety and trust in those around them, gradually rebuild their self-respect and grow in confidence in their ability to deal with the practical tasks, both in the refuge and in handling the situations they might meet in the future.

Women's accounts of domestic violence in Chapter 1 showed that a recurring theme was the dependence on one source of communication – the abuser – and growing isolation from other potential sources of support. Once free of these constraints, as they discussed in Chapter 4, it was important to them to reach out to others. They drew strength from a network of support systems, not only from the knowledge and expertise of refuge workers and volunteers, counsellors and group workers, but most importantly from the supportive community of other women within the refuge, where they were able both to give and receive practical and emotional support. Despite the tensions and conflicts which could arise, explored in Chapter 5, the experience of self-help and the flow of support between residents and, on occasion, former residents, was a key element of support and one which they valued highly. For a substantial number of women, this support and their discussions with other women had led to a growing under-standing of their own worth and validity as human beings, evolving into a further step in the recovery process beyond that which can be seen as taking place follow-ing bereavement; a changed perspective of themselves and their role in society, discussed in Chapter 6 and which I have called *Realignment.*

Not only will the practical and emotional needs of each woman change over the period of support, but she will also have specific needs relating to her own particular circumstances. The emotional impact of the losses she has sustained will mean that she is likely, at least in the initial period, to move forward and backward in her progress. Support, then, needs to be flexible in its approach and be continually reassessed as circumstances alter, but bearing in mind that the ultimate aim must be to enable a woman to take control of her life and make her own decisions.

The provision of this support cannot, in practical terms, be separated from the attitude which informs it and the way it is offered. In commenting on what was significant to them in the provision of support, women said that physical safety was their first priority. Once this was assured, it was always the underlying attitude with which support was given that women mentioned; being treated with respect, believed, feeling mentally secure and not judged, having time to talk and be really listened to and the emotional support of others. These qualities, discussed in detail in the preceding chapter, were those which gave them confidence in their own abilities and built on their existing strengths. It was also important to them to know that this attitude towards support meant that they were not 'abandoned' once they moved out. The assurance that respect and understanding would still be there for them should they need it, provided the reassurance that enabled them to make their own way forward.

A way of understanding

It may be thought contentious to see leaving an abusive relationship in terms of bereavement: openly mourning, to a limited extent, the loss which follows a death is generally considered nowadays to be socially acceptable. Domestic violence, on the other hand, as I learnt on many occasions during this research, is still a taboo and stigmatised subject. It could also be argued that bereavement is inappropriate as a model since, while the losses are deeply felt internally, externally the abuser is alive and all too often present, either in reality or as an invisible source of continuing fear and uncertainty.[2] This factor undoubtedly adds more complexity to the situation and to the pressures which make it difficult to move forward, as Jenny had found:

> Even though it's lessened from last year, he still has some tricks up his sleeve, that he plays every now and again, which, really, sort of, sets me back a little bit… Because it's ongoing with him, it's ongoing with me, really. I find that quite hard, because I just wish that it would be…that he would pack it in and that I could DEAL with all the things he's done and then start over. Just deal with it, really.

Nevertheless, what women say about their experiences clearly indicates that there is a definite and identifiable process; a model of loss and coping, which gives shape and meaning to their stay in the refuge and subsequent progress. Seeing this process in terms of bereavement gives a framework for understanding the losses involved and the practical and emotional stresses which accompany them. This framework is further strengthened by seeing the effects of domestic violence in terms of Maslow's ideas concerning human needs. This offers an approach which recognises the intrinsic need of human beings not just to survive, but to seek to belong to a community and to internalise feelings of self-worth and self-respect. It avoids any concept of stigma or victim blaming, recognises the positive and active efforts of women to care for themselves and their families and values the vital role played by the lay community in helping women to recover from the emotional impact of domestic violence and to establish lives free of violence and abuse. Such an approach provides a model that, for the majority of women who experience domestic violence, may well be more appropriate than that of post traumatic stress disorder (PTSD), leaving this diagnosis to be applied to the comparatively small number of women who require professional specialised medical assistance.

Bringing these two concepts together provides an integrated model of loss, trauma and recovery from domestic violence. It is neither prescriptive, nor does it impose expectations of behaviour, but it offers an explanatory framework for a fluid and dynamic process, centred on a woman's perspective of her experiences and acknowledging her active agency in defining her needs and working to achieve them.

One size will never fit all

This model of recovery, in its entirety, is unlikely to be appropriate for all women, since every woman's circumstances and the reasons behind her decisions will be different, but the insights it provides can be used to inform support provision, direct its focus in appropriate ways and enhance its effectiveness in the longer term.

Women come into a refuge for a variety of reasons. Some will be there to gain a breathing space before returning to the abusive situation, or to administer a brief shock to the abuser. These women are unlikely to want to move further along the path of leaving at this stage but can gain from the safety and confidentiality of the refuge. The awareness of support that can be gained from workers and other residents may increase confidence in making decisions, enabling them either to work to end the abuse within the relationship, or to decide to terminate it. Others may not finally have closed the door on the relationship and will be testing out their options and assessing their reactions and those of the abuser to the changed situation before coming to any firm decision. As with the previous group of women, understanding their position and difficulties in terms of Maslow's hierarchy of needs and relating this to the factors that women valued most in supporting them, shows the importance of providing a safe space, a supportive environment and time to think and talk about the relationship, their needs and those of their children.

A pattern of leaving and returning does not exclude the idea of experiencing loss. Women who had left and returned before told me that they had regarded each break as final. Indeed, some may have gone back again after they had talked to me. Realisation of actual and anticipated loss may well have played a part in these decisions. Faced with the need to wrestle with difficult emotional and practical problems and the social and economic disadvantages that they could see lying ahead of them, returning to the abusive relationship may well be seen as a valid and perhaps safer alternative, particularly if there is little prospect of continuing support within the wider community. Some women who come to a refuge may not feel able to respond to the type of support on offer, based on encouraging them to take control of their own lives rather than continuing to be told what to do, and may decide to leave, either for another type of assistance or to return to the relationship. Others may be unwilling to accept the restrictions necessary for safety, security and communal living and be asked, or choose, to leave.

For all of these groups, the process of recovery from domestic violence may be truncated or terminated, but may well be resumed at some future date. These women are facing difficult choices and decisions that will inevitably bring pain both to them and to others. It needs to be recognised that, as Maslow has pointed out, 'growth is often a painful process and may, for this reason, be shunned' (1987, p.xx). On the other hand, some women will already have established a plan of action in which the refuge plays a key but transient role. However planned their exit and future course of action, they too will be going through the process of recovery from loss, which needs to be taken into account in providing effective support.

In offering the right level of support to all these groups of women and to others who come to the refuge seeking shelter from domestic violence, workers constantly reassessed each individual woman's situation, which could be influenced by any of the above factors. As discussed in Chapter 7, they were committed to supporting women and putting their needs at the centre of their work, but the constant pressure involved could make this a stressful, frustrating and draining experience. It was essential for them to be able to receive support in their turn. This was most likely to be given by their close colleagues, but it was also important for them to feel valued and supported by their line manager and the organisation as a whole, where there needed to be a clear vision of the future, enabling workers to look beyond the day-to-day demands of the work.

Wider implications

This project drew on the experiences of women who had at some point in their lives stayed in a Women's Aid refuge, but the findings are equally likely to apply to women who have left or terminated an abusive relationship without entering a refuge. The insights that it presents can be of use to the statutory, professional and voluntary agencies who work in areas where issues of domestic violence may be involved, including health, social care, housing, education and employment. It offers a way of understanding the personal needs of women who may approach them, the differing sources of stress and the factors which will influence successful interventions.

Although the research involved mainly heterosexual women who had been subject to violence from male partners, the findings are also likely to be of use in approaching violence in same-sex relationships, female to male violence and violence in other family settings. There will be other specific issues in these situations that are likely to need further research, but the theories which inform this model – loss and the basic needs of human beings for safety, respect and connection to others – are of universal application and can guide and assist in the provision of effective support.

In working with any individual who is being subjected to domestic violence or abuse, it can be helpful to understand the way their confidence and sense of personal worth can become systematically eroded and the losses which will have to be faced if the decision to leave the relationship is made. This awareness can assist in understanding apparently irrational or contradictory behaviour, such as staying in or returning to the abuser (because it is, or seems to be, the safest or least unsafe option). Support giving, in these instances, can be enhanced by considering the factors which the women in this study saw as helping them to make successful transitions in their lives: the provision of a physically safe space, even if only for a few hours, being treated with respect, listened to and believed. Restoring connections to others and developing trust in the support on offer in this way will start to rebuild the self-esteem that will gradually enable them to take decisions and put them into practice.

Conclusions

The research presented here has been shaped by the voices of women who have experienced domestic violence and of workers with in-depth knowledge of their practical and emotional support needs. It provides a framework of understanding for others working in this field, both in refuges and in the wider community, explaining the reasons behind the changing nature of support needs and the twin stresses of practical and emotional pressures that women experience. In identifying the interlinked features and approaches which characterise effective support giving, it emphasises the need for this support work and the role it can play in assisting recovery from domestic violence.

For women who are or have been in a relationship characterised by violence and abuse, the research helps to provide meaning and give a sense of shape and holding to their experiences, enabling them to make sense of what can seem bewilderingly chaotic. It enables an individual woman to locate herself in a process which, while dynamic and flexible, has an ending. Giving this understanding is, in itself, of prime importance because it further contributes to her empowerment and ability to control her life. Talking informally to the women who took part in this study, they were surprised and relieved to hear that other women in refuges in other parts of the country felt the same as they did and that this was an understandable reaction to what they had gone through. Being 'normal' and seeing that there was a pathway through their present experiences was a significant milestone for them.

If women are to be successfully supported to recover from the effects of domestic violence, they need to be able to access practical support, advocacy and information. The research shows, however, that important though this is, it is not sufficient on its own. They also need the personal support and acceptance which will enable them to rebuild their self-respect and gain the confidence to live independently. The value of this complex and demanding work needs to be fully appreciated and properly funded, taking into account its one-to-one nature and the requirement for extended support within the community. Combining practical and emotional assistance in this way enhances the prospect of a successful transition to a new life for the woman and may also lessen future demands on health and social care provision and possible expensive crisis interventions.

Summary

- Women who leave an abusive relationship go through a phased process of loss, transition and recovery, similar to that which follows bereavement. These phases are fluid and dynamic, not linear, and women will move forward and back between them.

- Each phase has different tasks and requires both practical and emotional assistance. Support needs to be different for each woman and flexible in responding to her changing needs.

- The process of recovery is made more complex by the damage which domestic violence has caused to feelings of physical and mental safety, self-esteem and confidence. This can usefully be understood by seeing it in terms of Maslow's hierarchy of human needs.

- In rebuilding their lives, women prioritised the provision of a safe environment and an attitude to support work which respected them, believed their accounts of their experiences without judging them and provided time for them to talk and be genuinely heard.

- Support from other women with similar experiences provided a community which was able to offer understanding and reciprocal help.

- Applying this model of recovery from domestic violence offers a way of understanding support as needing to be structured and focused, requiring both practical and emotional help if it is to be effective.

- Aspects of this model can be applied in other situations where domestic violence is an issue, including those where a woman is still in the relationship, or adopting a pattern of leaving and returning while she explores her options.

- The theories which inform this model – loss and the basic needs of human beings for safety, respect and connections to others – are of universal application and can inform practice in other forms of intimate violence, including same-sex relationships and female violence to male partners.

Notes

1. Walby (2004).
2. Worden (1991) points out that 'uncertain' loss can exist in bereavement. He cites the case of soldiers missing in action and argues that this may make it difficult to bring mourning to a satisfactory conclusion, but does not preclude the need to try and come to grips with the situation.

Postscript

It is over 30 years since the first refuges were founded and domestic violence began to be seen as a problem within society that needed to be recognised and dealt with. Since then, persistent campaigning has raised awareness of the issues involved at a political level and there have been far-reaching changes in social, legal and economic policy and practice in this area. Popular media programmes have developed storylines on the subject and major documentaries have explored the context and impact of abuse.

Has this growth of awareness made a difference to what women want? This was the final question I posed to workers, many of whom had been involved in support work for more than ten years, some for more than 20. They all felt that the underlying desires had not changed at all:

> No. I think what the women want is safety, security for their children and to be able to get on with their lives. And that will probably go on for years and years and years and years. And want people to recognise what domestic violence is and what they're doing to them. And I don't think that will change. At all. (Katja)

> What women want is what women have always wanted. They want the violence to stop. (Frances)

> I think what women want is to be believed, and to be supported, and to have somewhere safe to live. And I think that's the same now and I think that will always be the same. (Jay)

Along with this unchanging aspect of domestic violence, however, there was also a consensus that women's expectations had changed; that women who contacted helplines or refuges wanted more out of life. Younger women were not as prepared to put up with abuse in the same way that previous generations had had to. They were more aware of what was abusive behaviour, that it was not acceptable and of the need to make changes in their lives. Daphne fully agreed with this view, but she felt that this change in attitude was also beginning to occur in older women as well:

> Are women saying 'for better, for worse – I've had enough of that. I've put up with "worse" for too long, I want a bit of "better" now'? So yes, I think there is a change. I think women are beginning to say…it's not about running away, it's about…what am I going to do with the rest of my life? How do I want it to be? How can I make it better than it has been? So yes, for me, I do see a change, a change in attitude.

Evidence supporting these comments comes from the accounts of the women who talked to me. They did, indeed, want safety and security, to be believed, to be supported to build new lives and for there to be a greater awareness of what domestic violence is and does. At the same time, as the comments of Amy and Amalie in Chapter 2 showed, there was for most of them a deep drive to make the new life better and to feel that they were accepted and worthy people in their own right.

Refuges are changing to meet the challenges that this new attitude demands. New forms of support have been developed; national and local helplines, advice and information centres and websites with protected access. Outreach and community-based services are being established to work alongside refuge provision, enabling women to stay in their own homes, if that is what they wish. Since this research was carried out, I have been back to the refuges which were involved. Major changes have taken place; new buildings, better facilities, more access to activities, additional staff and counsellors.

Yet there seems to be no diminution of the demand for these services. Every new refuge is full from the moment it opens its doors and there are usually waiting lists to enter them. The women who have told their stories in this book have shared their experiences in order to show the reality of domestic violence and to help other women to see that they can move out and move on. If they and others like them are to achieve their valid aspirations for a better life, it is clear that there is some way to go before their first and most essential requirement is met – for the violence and abuse to stop.

Appendix 1

Women's Aid Federation of England

Members of the Women's Aid Federation are the major providers in England of services to women who experience domestic violence. The federation and its sister organisations in Wales, Scotland and Northern Ireland developed from the Women's Movement of the 1960s and 1970s. Its organisational values include a commitment to collaborative working, mutual respect and support and to a feminist analysis of domestic violence. These federations, together with other groups concerned with women's services and projects, have been at the forefront of developing work with women, in addition to campaigning for changes to law, policies and practice in relation to domestic violence.

The Women's Aid approach to support for women rests on the belief that women are independent and equal individuals, competent and capable of defining their own problems, making choices and taking action, given a safe environment and support to access the information and resources they need. Its statement of key values reflects this and is derived from its roots in the women's movement:

- To believe women and children's experience of abuse
- To prioritise all abused women and children's safety and confidentiality
- To support empowerment and self-help so that women can gain control of their own lives
- To care for the emotional, developmental and educational needs of children affected by domestic violence [work with children and their mothers is discussed in Chapter 4]
- To challenge discrimination and promote equal opportunities
- To provide women for women services.

(Turner 1996, p.9)

Within these values, local groups have the flexibility to develop services and ways of working which are responsive to the needs of the women who approach them and the availability of financial and other resources.

Throughout the UK there is now a network of Women's Aid refuges providing safe accommodation and support for women and children. In recognition of specific cultural and practical needs of some women, there is limited specialist provision for women from minority communities, including a network of Asian refuges. Some of these groups provide the only community-specific refuge in the UK; that for Jewish women is unique in Europe. (See Chapter 2 for a fuller discussion of the factors which may influence a woman's choice of refuge, where such a choice exists.) A small number of other specialist refuges exist, for example, for women without children, for those who have been sexually abused, or for women who have learning difficulties. Provision in refuges for women with limited mobility, with other physical problems, or with dependency problems in addition to those caused by domestic violence, although gradually increasing, is in general very limited. Although a member of Women's Aid, Refuge operates its own provision. There are also specialist refuges for black and Asian women which operate outside the Women's Aid network. Additionally, there are a growing number of refuges provided directly by housing associations, many of whom follow the Women's Aid model of support. A freephone 24-hour National Domestic Violence Helpline (0808 2000 247) is run in partnership between Women's Aid and Refuge and provides a link to the refuge network, as well as offering help and support to women experiencing domestic violence.

In addition to working with women who enter a refuge, projects have always offered some form of support to residents who are rehoused in the local area and have recognised the need to provide assistance and advice on a wider basis to women in the community who may be experiencing or have experienced domestic abuse. These services may be referred to as outreach, resettlement or aftercare, or floating support and are expanding to meet the needs of women who are unwilling or unable to enter a refuge, those who are able to stay in their own homes and those who need support within the relationship.

The Research Project

About the project

The broad aims of the research were:

1. To find out what sort of support was available to women who left an abusive relationship and came to a refuge run by members of the Women's Aid Federation of England.

2. To examine the approach to service delivery that was adopted.

3. To ask past and present service users about their experiences of support, including what was available, how it was delivered, positive and negative aspects and to identify any unmet needs.

These issues were last explored in detail over 20 years ago and in view of the social and political changes which had taken place over that period, together with the way policy and practice were continuing to evolve, it was thought essential to assess the present situation. This research was initiated as a collaborative project between the Women's Aid Federation of England (WAFE) and the Violence Against Women Research Group (VAWRG) which forms a part of the School for Policy Studies at the University of Bristol. As it progressed, this base widened to include participation at a variety of levels from groups and individuals within the sponsoring organisation.

Three refuge groups were collaborative partners in this research. Each of them, at the time, operated two refuge houses. They were drawn from a number of groups who expressed interest in the project as a result of an article in the newsletter of the organisation. Between them, they encompassed a wide diversity of settings: urban and rural catchment areas, geographical locations, varying socioeconomic and demographic characteristics and the services they offered. Explicitly specialist refuges were excluded because of the additional cultural and social factors which would need to be taken into account. The refuge groups did, however, include one serving a variety of minority community groups and these were also well represented in the workshops which helped to shape the research. (See Designing the Research for further details on this.) This input was further enhanced by an extended interview with workers at a specialist Asian refuge.

Theoretical approach

The research was carried out using an approach based on participative action research (PAR) informed by feminist research practice. PAR is based on a genuine and open collaboration between the researcher and those who take part in the research, stresses the value of lived experience and aims to produce practical knowledge which is directly useful to the participants (Reason 1994). 'Feminist research practice' (Kelly 1988, p.4), which can be seen more as a mindset than one of methods used (which are not in themselves feminist), is similarly concerned to work with the participants, seeing them as experts in their own lives and emphasises the need to be aware of issues of power and control within the research context.

These views were consistent with the values and approach adopted by Women's Aid (detailed in Appendix 1) and with my personal belief in the value of collaborative research as producing knowledge that is grounded in real life experience, owned by the participants, and of practical use to them.

Designing the research

With support from the national office of WAFE and the VAWRG, I developed a framework for the research, based on the aims outlined above. This was then the subject of a widespread consultation process within Women's Aid, both at workshops held at the annual conferences and with the individuals and groups who had responded to the original article. Those involved worked in a variety of service provision areas, including refuges, outreach and resettlement and came from a diversity of cultural backgrounds and locations across England. Much of this input came from women who identified themselves as current or former refuge users. Their comments and ideas were used to further define the aims and objectives of the research and the way it should be carried out, and to assist in the drafting of topic guides, information sheets and feedback forms. Each of the groups that had agreed to participate in the project then held detailed discussions with me on the research and any particular questions or issues which they wanted to be explored within the context of the research. We also discussed how and when the work was to be carried out, tailoring it to the physical resources of the group and their preferred way of working.

Access

Women's Aid and other women's groups working in the field of domestic violence have always been extremely sensitive to being 'used' or exploited by outsiders, including academics, or those who may not be in sympathy with their ideas and values. A number of the groups and individuals who contacted me expressed similar apprehension and uncertainty over becoming involved. For some, recent and past experiences had made them extremely wary of giving access to researchers, both in the interests of their residents and of the organisation. All of the groups who finally became involved in this research needed to meet and talk to me at length to satisfy themselves that the research would not be exploitative and that it would be of use to them as well as to WAFE. They also needed to feel able to work with me, to be confident in my personal style, motivation and research abilities and that they had sufficient resources to be able to work as partners in the research process. Whatever their organisational structure, all the groups operated on a consultative basis and needed time to consult, discuss and reach a consensus decision on whether I should be invited to carry out the research, how it should be carried out and the questions they wanted answered. Workers also discussed the proposed research with residents at house meetings to gain their views. This preparatory work meant that mutual confidence and understanding developed over this period, which grew further during the time of the research and in subsequent 'feedback' visits. The enthusiasm and involvement of everyone who took part in this research was a major factor in its effectiveness and to the rich and detailed findings which emerged.

Contact with residents was initially mediated through the workers. Because of the temporary nature of refuge accommodation, some of the residents who had originally talked over the project had moved out and new families had arrived. Workers discussed the research with the residents again shortly before the field work was due to commence, gave them written details of what would be involved and invited them to participate if they wished. Since my visits extended over a week at a time, I was able to be present in the refuge for long periods during the day and evening. This meant that residents as well as workers could approach me directly, talk to me informally and decide for themselves if they wished to take part in the research, or to withdraw if they had previously accepted the invitation to participate. Contact with ex-residents was also made through the refuge but was markedly less successful.

Methods

At each refuge I examined the documents on policy and practice to gain understanding of the approach used, identify any extra areas to explore and to gather basic statistical information without imposing extra burdens on workers. At the same time, I carried out semi-structured interviews with residents, former residents and workers directly involved in working with women. (A précis of the topic guide used is in Appendix 3.) Additional interviews also took place with specialist workers such as child support staff and counsellors, volunteer staff and managers. Semi-structured interviews were chosen as the main method of gathering information because they provided a flexible structure to enable participants to reflect on their experiences of support, both positive and negative, and to talk about the things that were important to them, while making sure that the areas which had been identified by the collaborative process were covered. All those involved were encouraged to think broadly about issues and how they might affect other women as well as themselves. Interview timing was flexible, but lasted, in general, between 45 minutes and one hour. The timing was arranged to suit the needs of the women and could be (and was regularly) changed as necessary to cope with unforeseen events. Interviews were tape recorded except where this was not acceptable to the participant and an interview with one woman who was not able to communicate verbally was carried out in writing, signs and paraphrasing. (Workers were not sure if her speech had been affected by the trauma of domestic violence, or some other condition, but were confident that her other faculties were unimpaired and she was eager to be included in the work.)

Research at each refuge was carried out over a period of weeks and enabled workers and, in communal refuges, residents, to get used to me being there. This meant that I could observe the interactions which took place in the communal areas and public offices and become involved in informal discussions on a wide range of topics. Women, workers and volunteers, in becoming more relaxed about talking to me, added comments and insights to their original interviews in one-to-one exchanges and in groups. These exchanges and general impressions were recorded in field notes. Although I carried out small tasks to assist workers and volunteers, and was accepted and included in general conversations by residents, this did not in my view reach the level of involvement that could be described as participant observation. Not only did I lack the experience and training of the workers and volunteers, but also I could not fully participate in the world of the residents. The essential difference between us was clearly brought home to me in this excerpt from my field notes:

Liz (resident): You off now, then?

Me: Yes, down to the station.

Liz: It's all right for you. You can go home. We can never go home.

The data that were collected, then, came from documentary evidence, interviews and observation, together with informal discussions with individuals and small groups. I transcribed the taped interviews and analysed them, together with the other sources of data, using the themes suggested by the research objectives and the topics which emerged from the interviews as being important to those taking part. These were grouped into broader areas and set within the context of each individual group in order to produce a report for their use, with particular emphasis on the aspects that they had wanted examined. Data from all three groups were reanalysed to provide a comprehensive report for the national office of WAFE. Copies of this also went to the individual groups and the findings were additionally disseminated at conference and other presentations.

Ethics

'Ethics is always about fair and honest dealings' (Kellehear 1993, p.14). Codes of practice that seek to clarify this simple statement and provide minimum guidelines for research emphasise informed consent, avoidance of harm to the participant and consideration of their rights, privacy and confidentiality and safety issues. Ethical practice on this project followed the general guidelines of the British Sociological Association (2002) together with those of the British Association for Counselling and Psychotherapy (2002) which stress the duty to consider and carefully protect the rights of participants and the need for personal integrity, respect and resilience on the part of the researcher. These aspects are particularly important when the research focus is on women who have experienced domestic violence, given the physical and psychological consequences to them and the potential for harm which unconsidered research might present.

The two aspects of ethical research practice which I considered of particular importance in carrying out individual interviews (whether with service users, workers and volunteers) were the obtaining of 'informed consent' and the duty of care towards participants. Informed consent should involve clear understanding of the purpose of the research, the use that will be made of the information and the right to privacy, safety and confidentiality. All potential interviewees received a letter out-lining the purpose of the research, the areas to be covered, details about the conduct of the interview and the ways in which the information might be used. A telephone number was included to enable any concerns to be talked over directly with me. Those who expressed interest were given more detailed information about the research. At the time of interview, the main points concerning consent were reiterated and a brief note confirming the right to confidentiality and anonymity, to stop the interview, speak off the record and to have a copy of the tape or notes were also supplied and discussed. There was an opportunity to ask any questions about these or any other aspect of the research before the interview commenced. The mixture of written and oral information was given because for some respondents English was not a first language,[1] others had difficulty with reading and writing and a few had minor learning difficulties. At the beginning of each interview I also mentioned the possible revelation of information on which I would not feel able to maintain confi-dentiality, such as child protection issues, or the possibility of self-harm or harm to others. I emphasised that although action might need to be taken by workers, this would be discussed first with the informant.

In carrying out in-depth interviews, informed consent cannot be a 'one-off' process, since unforeseen issues may arise during the course of the interview and sen-sitive and potentially damaging information may be revealed which pose moral and ethical dilemmas for the researcher and stress and anxiety for the interviewee. Consent, therefore, needed to be monitored throughout the interview and if neces-sary I would check with the participant if she wanted to continue, and if so whether this was to be 'on' or 'off' the record.

In any research there is, or should be, a duty of care towards participants, requir-ing awareness and sensitivity both during the interview and afterwards. Not only may interviewees reveal information that they had not intended to divulge, even giving the interview may result in an unexpected emotional impact either at the time, or at a later date. These possibilities were discussed in advance and I took with me details of the available external and internal support systems at national and local levels, which could be passed on as necessary. This provision was not simply for resi-dents, since many refuge and other Women's Aid workers are themselves women who have experienced domestic violence. Interview material of this nature may also be a source of stress and anxiety for the researcher, particularly when being trusted with sensitive and potentially damaging information, and for this reason I put together a support network to meet my own needs in this respect. Because of the nature of the research, physical safety was an important consideration, both for my informants and for me. Not only did this involve keeping addresses, phone numbers and sensitive material under strict security, it also required vigilance in approaching buildings, method of leaving and mode of public transport, together with a telephone check-in system.

Ethical practice also extends to the organisation where research is being carried out. Refuges are often overcrowded and chronically underfunded with workers under extreme pressure to cope with the demands being made on them. Researchers need to be aware of this and to treat the organisation with respect, appreciating its knowledge and acting responsibly in the conduct of the research. I also felt that it was important to be able to give something back – to ensure that the groups did not feel that their involvement had not resulted in any advantages for them. Reciprocity was achieved by the individual reports given to each group and by the production of broad based research of general application to Women's Aid groups and to the federation. This is already proving of use to the case study groups and has also been shared with other practitioners and service users within Women's Aid. In addition, some aspects of the research data have been actively used in respect of political lobbying and as evidence at an industrial tribunal. I have also been able to act as a conduit for information, ideas and contacts between and outside the groups and continue to do so. There seems also to be an intangible sense of pride at having worked on the research, a sense of involvement and ownership. All of the groups were happy to be identified by name as having taken part in the research.

Participants – residents and former residents

A total of 17 interviews were held with residents. Attempts by workers to contact ex-residents were much less successful and it was only possible for me to interview six women from two of the refuge groups. One of these had left the refuge five years ago, two left between 12 and 18 months previously, two had moved out five months previously and one had moved out three months earlier. In discussing this situation with me, residents and workers suggested that for many women there was just too much to attend to immediately on leaving the refuge and that women might subsequently want to move on and forget details of their stay, however satisfactory it had been at the time. It could also be argued that they were being approached by an unknown person (albeit with the backing of the refuge) and that they were concerned about their own safety and wary of possible exploitation. No more than two attempts were made to make contact with any former resident, to avoid any appearance of harassment and to minimise any possible danger to the women if they had returned to an abusive relationship.

Three of those interviewed identified themselves as coming from minority community groups. Two women said that they had physical impairments and one of these, together with another woman, was informally assessed by workers as having slight learning difficulties. Two of the women said that they were lesbians, one of whom was escaping male violence and the other abuse from a female partner. The women all came from widely differing backgrounds, life histories and roles, providing perspectives on support and refuge life from their individual viewpoints. Their ages ranged from 21 to 68, distributed as in Figure A2.1.

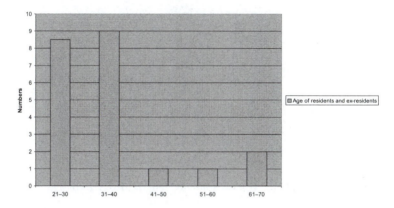

Figure A2.1 Residents and ex-residents by age

At the time of their stay, 65 per cent of both residents and ex-residents were, or had been pregnant or accompanied by one or more children, most of whom were under five, as shown in Figure A2.2. Five women had had adult children who were already living away from home, but seven women had been unable to bring some or all of their children into the refuge with them. These children were either with another family member (usually the perpetrator) or being looked after by the local authority, either in their home area or in that of the refuge.

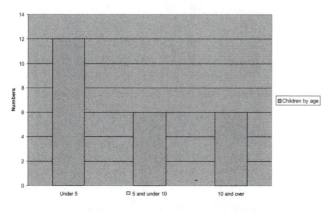

Figure A2.2 Children by age

For 15 of my informants (65%) this was their first visit to a refuge, although they may have stayed with family or friends on previous occasions of leaving and some had stayed a short while in refuges near their homes before coming to the present refuge. Of the remainder, six had made two to three visits, one had been to five refuges and one thought she had been to at least seven. The length of time they had been in their present refuge at the time of interview is shown in Figure A2.3.

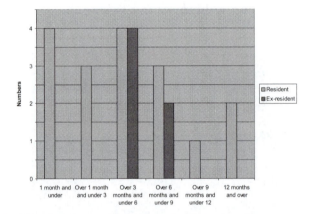

Figure A2.3 Residents' and ex-residents' length of stay in refuge

Women were also asked how far they had travelled to reach the refuge. Although this did not appear to be directly relevant to the research on support, it was considered to be important because of the possibility that local authorities might be willing to provide funding only for refuges within their areas or in adjacent localities, where arrangements might well be considered to be reciprocal. As shown in Figure A2.4, almost half of the women had travelled more than 100 miles to reach the refuge they were in at the time of interview and four had come well over 300 miles. The proportion of local residents to women who had travelled from outside the immediate area of the refuge was broadly similar across all three groups: 1:6 in two of them and 1:7 in the third.

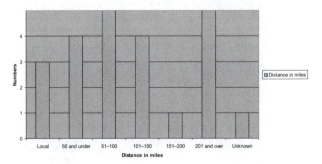

Figure A2.4 Distance travelled to refuge by informants

Participants – workers

A total of 23 interviews were held with workers directly involved with supporting residents and ex-residents. One of these had previously been a resident and contributed in both contexts. The relevant proportions of staff interviewed by role are shown in Figure A2.5.

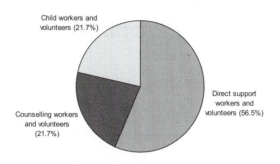

Figure A2.5 Workers directly involved with supporting residents and ex-residents

Of the overall number of workers and volunteers interviewed (39), five volunteered the fact that they had had direct personal experience of domestic violence. This continuing involvement has remained a constant feature of Women's Aid.

Note

1. Arrangements had been made for independent translators to be available for any woman who preferred to communicate in her first language, but this resource was not called upon. One interview was partially conducted in French. Crèche and playroom facilities had also been negotiated to enable women with young children to participate.

Précis of Topic Guide for Interviews with Past and Present Service Users

1. Background
    - Personal details, including age, details and whereabouts of any children.
    - Previous visits to refuges or other safe accommodation.
    - Length of present stay.

2. Initial contact
    - How did you hear about the refuge?
    - Circumstances of leaving, details of reception at the refuge.
    - How did you feel about the reception process?
    - Where there any gaps, or additional provision you would have liked?

3. Continuation
    - What support was available inside the refuge? (included formal and informal sources, counselling and group work and peer support)
    - Which of these did you access?
    - What was of most value, helpful/not helpful and why?
    - Was there less support after a while?
    - Did you become involved in running the refuge? (helping to welcome new residents, attendance at and involvement in house meetings)
    - Did you take part in any other activities? (personal development, group activities, education, outings)
    - Grievance and disciplinary procedures – awareness, utilisation.
    - Where there any gaps in service provision?
    - What else would you have liked in the way of help from the refuge?
    - Do you think the refuge meets the needs of women with different abilities?

4. Later contact

- When did you leave the refuge?
- If you went back (to the abusive partner) would you not have done so with different support?
- Were plans for the future made with you before you left the refuge?
- Was there any resettlement/follow-up? How did this work? Was it helpful/not helpful?
- Did you get support from other sources after you left? What were they?
- Are you still in contact with the refuge? Or the women that you met there?
- Were there any other ways you would have liked the refuge to help you after you left?

5. Satisfaction

- What was valued most and what were the difficulties?
- Did you feel you were in control? (listened to, involved in own care plan, how the refuge operated)
- Is there anything this refuge should be working to improve?
- The best thing was…
- The worst thing was…

6. Experience of refuge(s) not associated with Women's Aid

- Managed by? When were you there?
- Was it different? In what way?

7. Missing areas

- What kind of things do you think refuges should be there for?
- Are there other things that you would like refuges to be able to do?
- What would be your hope?

As indicated in Appendix 2, preliminary discussions with each of the groups had revealed particular concerns which they wanted the research to address. Topic guides for each group reflected these individual concerns and each, therefore, varied slightly from the others. The main areas of enquiry remained the same and this précis is broadly representative of the areas explored.

The topic guide for workers covered the same ground as that for residents and former residents but from a worker's perspective. It also asked about their own background, experience and training, how they obtained personal support, key issues within the local organisation and the factors which held them back in their work. They were also invited to explore their hopes for the future of the refuge and their views as to whether the needs of women had changed. Specialist workers were asked about their particular field and its relationship to the rest of the group. Managerial interviews discussed the organisation and structure of the group, as well as an overview of the work.

Resource Materials

Below is a small selection of the groups and organisations offering support and information to those who experience domestic violence and abuse. It is a good idea to remind individuals that they need to be cautious when accessing any of the websites from a computer which their abuser has access to. Many of the sites contain information on actions that can be taken to minimise the chance that access might be discovered.

National 24-hour Domestic Violence Helpline
Tel: 0808 2000 247 (minicom available)
Websites: Refuge (www.refuge.org.uk); Women's Aid (www.womensaid.org.uk)
Run in partnership between Women's Aid and Refuge, freephone service for support, advice, information and access to a range of other services, including safe houses and outreach. Callers can be signposted to many other sources of help to meet individual requirements.

Northern Ireland Women's Aid Helpline
Tel: 0800 917 1414
Website: www.niwaf.org

Scottish Women's Aid
Tel: 0800 027 1234
Website: www.scottishwomensaid.co.uk

Welsh Women's Aid
Tel: 0800 8010 800
Website: www.welshwomensaid.org.

Broken Rainbow
Tel: 0845 260 4460
Website: www.broken-rainbow.org.uk
Service for lesbian, gay men, bi- or transgendered people.

Rape Crisis
Tel: see local telephone numbers
Website: www.rapecrisis.org.uk
National organisation operating local centres for women who have experienced rape or sexual abuse. Has a link showing local services for male victims.

Southall Black Sisters
Tel: 020 8571 9595
Website: www.southallblacksisters.org.uk
Specialist advice and support for Asian and Afro-Caribbean women suffering violence and abuse.

Tulip Group
Tel: 0151 637 6363
Support for parents experiencing abuse from their children.

Victim Support
Tel: see local telephone numbers
Website: www.victimsupport.org.uk
Service for the victims of crime, and those who are acting as witnesses in court.

Children's services

Childline
Tel: 0800 1111
Website: www.childline.org.uk
Confidential counselling service for children. The website has a weblink for children and young people to use.

The Hideout
Website: www.thehideout.org.uk
Link from Women's Aid for children and young people.

NSPCC Child Protection Helpline
Tel: 0808 800 5000
Website: www.nspcc.org.uk
Advice and information on parenting related issues. Website has a weblink for children to use.

Services for the elderly

Elder Abuse Response Line
Tel: 0808 808 8141
Website: www.elderabuse.org.uk
Confidential helpline providing information and emotional support to the elderly and their carers and to professionals on all aspects of elder abuse.

Services for men experiencing domestic violence

Barnsley Domestic Violence Group
Tel: 01226 249 800
Website: www.barnsleydvg.org
Helpline for anyone experiencing violence, but with specific help for men.

Mankind
Tel: 0870 794 4124
Website: www.mankind.org.uk
Advice, information and support for male victims.

Services for male perpetrators of domestic violence

Respect National Association for Domestic Violence Perpetrator Programmes and Associated Support Services
Tel: 01324 485595
Website: www.changeweb.org.uk/respect

Everyman Project
Tel: 0207 263 8884
Website: www.everymanproject.co.uk
Service providing counselling and anger management services to men wishing to end abusive behaviour.

References

American Psychiatric Association (APA, 1980) *Diagnostic and Statistical Manual of Mental Disorders*, 3rd edn. Washington, DC: American Psychiatric Association.

Amiel, S. and Heath, I. (eds) (2003) *Family Violence in Primary Care.* Oxford: Oxford University Press.

Arnold, L. and Magill, A. (2000) *Making Sense of Self-Harm.* Abergavenny: Basement Project.

Atkinson, S. (2005) 'Internet technology: How safe is it?' *SAFE 16*, 10–13.

Ball, M. (1994) *Funding Refuge Services: A Study of Refuge Support Services for Women and Children Experiencing Domestic Violence.* Bristol: Women's Aid Federation of England.

Barron, J. (2002) *Five Years On: A Review of Legal Protection from Domestic Violence.* Bristol: Women's Aid Federation of England.

Barron, J. (2004) *Struggle to Survive: Challenges for Delivering Services on Mental Mealth, Substance Misuse and Domestic Violence.* Bristol: Women's Aid Federation of England.

Batsleer, J., Burman, E., Chantler, K., McIntosh, H., Pantling, K., Smailes, S. and Warner, S. (2002) *Domestic Violence and Minoritisation – Supporting Women to Independence.* Manchester: Manchester Metropolitan University.

Bewley, S., Friend, J. and Mezey, G. (eds) (1997) *Violence against Women.* London: Royal College of Obstetricians and Gynaecologists.

Binney, V., Harkell, G. and Nixon, J. (1981) *Leaving Violent Men.* Bristol: Women's Aid Federation of England.

Bond, T. (2000) *Standards and Ethics for Counselling in Action*, 2nd edn. London: Sage.

Bossy, J. and Coleman, S. (2000) *Womanspeak: Parliamentary Domestic Violence Internet Consultation.* Bristol: Women's Aid Federation of England.

Bowlby, J. (1980) *Attachment and Loss, Vol. 3: Loss, Sadness and Depression.* London: Hogarth Press.

British Association for Counselling and Psychotherapy (BACP, 2002) *Ethical Framework for Good Practice in Counselling and Psychotherapy.* Rugby: BACP.

British Sociological Association (BSA, 2002) *Statement of Ethical Practice.* London: BSA.

Butler, S. and Wintram, C. (1991) *Feminist Groupwork.* London: Sage.

Cascardi, M., O'Leary, K. and Schlee, K. (1999) 'Co-occurrence and correlates of post-traumatic stress disorder and major depression in physically abused women.' *Journal of Family Violence 14*, 3, 227–249.

Charles, N. (1994) 'The housing needs of women and children escaping domestic violence.' *Journal of Social Policy 23*, 4, 465–487.

Clifton, J. (1985) 'Refuges and self help.' In N. Johnson (ed.) *Marital Violence.* London: Routledge and Kegan Paul.

Coleman, G. and Guildford, A. (2001) 'Threshold Women's Mental Health Initiative: Striving to keep women's mental health issues on the agenda.' *Feminist Review 68*, 173–180.

Croft, S. and Beresford, P. (1989) 'User-involvement, citizenship and social policy.' *Critical Social Policy 9*, 2, 5–18.

Davis, C. (2003) *Housing Associations – Re-housing Women Leaving Domestic Violence: New Challenges and Good Practice.* Bristol: Policy Press.

Delahay, L. and Turner, A. (1998) *Refuge Services: Meeting the Needs of Women and Children?* Bristol: Women's Aid Federation of England.

Denzin, N. and Lincoln, Y. (eds) (1994) *Handbook of Qualitative Research.* London: Sage.

Dobash, R. and Dobash, R. (1979) *Violence Against Wives: A Case Against the Patriarchy.* New York: Free Press.

Dobash, R. and Dobash, R. (1992) *Women, Violence and Social Change.* London: Routledge.

Dobash, R. and Dobash, R. (2000) 'The politics and policies of responding to violence against women.' In J. Hanmer and C. Itzin with S. Quaid and D. Wigglesworth (eds) *Home Truths about Domestic Violence.* London: Routledge.

Dobash, R., Dobash, R., Cavanagh, K. and Lewis, R. (2000) *Changing Violent Men.* London: Sage.

Dutton, M. (1992) *Empowering and Healing the Battered Woman: A Model for Assessment and Intervention.* New York: Springer.

Feltham, C. (2000) 'An introduction to counselling and psychotherapy.' In S. Palmer (ed.) *Introduction to Counselling and Psychotherapy.* London: Sage.

Gelles, R. and Loseke, D. (eds) (1993) *Current Controversies on Family Violence.* London: Sage.

Glass, D. (1995) *All My Fault: Why Women Don't Leave Abusive Men.* London: Virago.

Golding, J. (1999) 'Intimate partner violence as a risk factor for mental disorders: a meta-analysis.' *Journal of Family Violence 14*, 2, 19–132.

Hague, G., Mullender, A., Aris, R. and Dear, W. (2002) *Abused Women's Perspectives: Responsiveness and Accountability of Domestic Violence and Inter-agency Initiatives.* Bristol: School for Policy Studies, University of Bristol.

Hanmer, J. and Itzin, C. with Quaid, S. and Wigglesworth, D. (eds) (2000) *Home Truths about Domestic Violence.* London: Routledge.

Harwin, N. (1997) 'Understanding women's experiences of abuse.' In S. Bewley, J. Friend and G. Mezey (eds) *Violence against Women.* London: Royal College of Obstetricians and Gynaecologists.

Heath, I. (2003) 'The meaning of domestic violence.' In S. Amiel and I. Heath (eds) *Family Violence in Primary Care.* Oxford: Oxford University Press.

Herman, J. (1992) *Trauma and Recovery.* London: Pandora.

Hester, M. and Pearson, C. (1998) *From Periphery to Centre – Domestic Violence in Work with Abused Children.* Bristol: Policy Press.

Hester, M. with Scott, J. (2000) *Women in Abusive Relationships: Groupwork and Agency Support.* Sunderland: University of Sunderland.

Hester, M. and Westmarland, N. (2005) *Tackling Domestic Violence – Effective Interventions and Approaches.* Home Office Research Study no. 290. London: Home Office.

Hoff, L. (1990) *Battered Women as Survivors.* London: Routledge.

Home Office (2004) *Developing Domestic Violence Strategies – A Guide for Partnerships.* Accessed September 2005 from http://www.crimereduction.gov.uk/domesticviolence46.htm

Humphreys, C. and Joseph, S. (2004) 'Domestic Violence and the Politics of Trauma.' *Women's Studies International Forum 27*, 559–570.

Humphreys, C. and Thiara, R. (2002) *Routes to Safety*. Bristol: Women's Aid Federation of England.

Humphreys, C. and Thiara, R. (2003) 'Mental health and domestic violence: "I call it symptoms of abuse".' *British Journal of Social Work 33*, 209–226.

Johnson, N. (ed.) (1985) *Marital Violence*. London: Routledge and Kegan Paul.

Jones, A., Pleace, N. and Quilgars, D. (2002) *Firm Foundations: An Evaluation of the Shelter 'Homeless to Home' Service*. London: Shelter.

Kellehear, A. (1993) *The Unobtrusive Researcher*. Sydney: Allen and Unwin.

Kelly, L. (1988) *Surviving Sexual Violence*. Cambridge: Polity Press.

Kelly, L. and Humphreys, C. (2001) 'Supporting women and children in their communities.' In J. Taylor-Browne (ed.) *What Works in Reducing Domestic Violence: A Comprehensive Guide for Professionals*. London: Whiting and Birch.

Kirkwood, C. (1993) *Leaving Abusive Partners*. London: Sage.

Kingston, P. and Penhale, B. (eds) (1995) *Family Violence and the Caring Professions*. London: Macmillan.

Lempert, L. (1996) 'Women's strategies for survival: developing agency in abusive relationships.' *Journal of Family Violence 11*, 3, 269–289.

Levison, D. and Harwin, N. (2001) 'Accommodation provision.' In J.Taylor-Browne (ed.) *What Works in Reducing Domestic Violence: A Comprehensive Guide for Professionals*. London: Whiting and Birch.

Lloyd, S. (1995) 'Social work and domestic violence.' In P. Kingston and B. Penhale (eds) *Family Violence and the Caring Professions*. London: Macmillan.

Lodge, S., Goodwin, J. and Pearson, C. (2001) *Domestic Violence in Devon: A Mapping Exercise*. Exeter: Devon County Council/Devon and Cornwall Constabulary.

McGee, C. (2000a) *Childhood Experiences of Domestic Violence*. London: Jessica Kingsley Publishers.

McGee, C. (2000b) 'Childhood experiences of domestic violence.' In J. Hanmer and C. Itzin with S. Quaid and D. Wigglesworth (eds) *Home Truths about Domestic Violence*. London: Routledge.

McGibbon, A., Cooper, L. and Kelly, L. (1989) *What Support?* London: Hammersmith and Fulham Council.

Malos, E. and Hague, G. (1993) *Domestic Violence and Housing: Local Authority Responses to Women and Children Escaping Violence in the Home*. Bristol: Women's Aid Federation of England/School of Applied Social Studies, University of Bristol.

Mama, A. (1996) *The Hidden Struggle: Statutory and Voluntary Responses to Violence Against Black Women in the Home*. London: Whiting and Birch.

Maslow, A. (1987) *Motivation and Personality*, 3rd edn. London: Harper and Row. (First published 1954.)

Mirrlees-Black, C. (1999) *Domestic Violence: Findings from a New British Crime Survey Self Completed Questionnaire*. London: Home Office.

Mooney, J. (1993) *The Hidden Figure: Domestic Violence in North London*. Middlesex University Centre for Criminology, School of Sociology and Social Policy.

Mooney, J. (2000) 'Revealing the hidden figure of domestic violence.' In J. Hanmer and C. Itzin with S. Quaid and D. Wigglesworth (eds) *Home Truths about Domestic Violence*. London: Routledge.

Morley, R. (2000) 'Domestic violence and housing.' In J. Hanmer and C. Itzin with S. Quaid and D. Wigglesworth (eds) *Home Truths about Domestic Violence*. London: Routledge.

Morris, L. (2001) 'Emotional literacy for kids.' *Counselling and Psychotherapy Journal 12*, 8, 15–18.

Mullender, A. and Morley, R. (1994) 'Context and content of a new agenda.' In A. Mullender and R. Morley (eds) *Children Living with Domestic Violence*. London: Whiting and Birch.

Mullender, A. and Morley, R. (eds) (1994) *Children Living with Domestic Violence*. London: Whiting and Birch.

Mullender, A. and Ward, D. (1991) *Self Directed Groupwork: Users Take Action for Empowerment*. London: Whiting and Birch.

Murphy, P. (1997) 'Recovering from the effects of domestic violence: implications for welfare reform policy.' *Law and Policy 19*, 169–182.

Murray Parkes, C. (1986) *Bereavement: Studies of Grief in Adult Life*. London: Penguin.

Murray Parkes, C., Relf, M. and Couldrick, A. (1996) *Counselling in Terminal Care and Bereavement*. Leicester: British Psychological Society.

Pahl, J. (1978) *A Refuge for Battered Women*. London: HMSO.

Pahl, J. (1985) 'Refuges for battered women: ideology and action.' *Feminist Review 19*, 25–43.

Palmer, S. (ed.) (2000) *Introduction to Counselling and Psychotherapy*. London: Sage.

Parmar, A., Sampson, A. and Diamond, A. (2005) *Tackling Domestic Violence: Providing Advocacy and Support to Survivors of Domestic Violence*. Home Office Development and Practice Report no. 34. London: Home Office.

Povey, D. (ed.) (2004) *Crime in England and Wales 2002/2003: Supplementary Volume 1: Homicide and Gun Crime*. London: Home Office.

Radford, J., Friedberg, M. and Harne, L. (eds) (1999) *Women, Violence and Strategies for Action*. Maidenhead: Open University Press.

Rai, D. and Thiara, R. (1997) *Redefining Spaces: The Needs of Black Women and Children in Refuge Support Services and Black Workers in Women's Aid*. Bristol: Women's Aid Federation of England.

Reason, P. (1994) 'Three approaches to participative inquiry.' In N. Denzin and Y. Lincoln (eds) *Handbook of Qualitative Research*. London: Sage.

Rose, H. (1985) 'Women's refuges: creating new forms of welfare?' In C. Ungerson (ed.) *Women and Social Policy*. London: Macmillan.

Shuchter, S. and Zisook, S. (1993) 'The course of normal grief.' In M. Stroebe, W. Stroebe and R. Hansson (eds) *Handbook of Bereavement: Theory, Research and Intervention*. Cambridge: Cambridge University Press.

Skinner, T. (1999) 'Feminist strategy and tactics.' In J. Radford, M. Friedberg and L. Harne (eds) *Women, Violence and Strategies for Action*. Buckingham: Open University Press.

Stanko, E. (2000) *The Day to Count. A Snapshot of the Impact of Domestic Violence in the UK*. Retrieved 20 October 2000 from http//www.domesticviolencedata.org/5_researc/count/.htm.

Stanko, E., Crisp, D., Hale, C. and Lucraft, H. (1998) *Counting the Costs: Estimating the Impact of Domestic Violence in the London Borough of Hackney*. Uxbridge: Brunel University, Centre for Criminal Justice Research.

Stark, E. and Flitcraft, A. (1996) *Women at Risk: Domestic Violence and Women's Health*. London: Sage.

Stevens, K. (1997) 'The role of the accident and emergency department.' In S. Bewley, J. Friend and G. Mezey (eds) *Violence against Women.* London: Royal College of Obstetricians and Gynaecologists.

Stroebe, M. and Schut, H. (1999) 'The dual process model of coping with bereavement: rationale and description.' *Death Studies 23,* 197–224.

Stroebe, M., Stroebe, W. and Hansson, R. (eds) (1993) *Handbook of Bereavement: Theory, Research and Intervention.* Cambridge: Cambridge University Press.

Taylor-Browne, J. (ed.) (2001) *What Works in Reducing Domestic Violence: A Comprehensive Guide for Professionals.* London: Whiting and Birch.

Trevithick, P. (2000) *Social Work Skills: A Practice Handbook.* Maidenhead: Open University Press.

Turner, A. (1996) *Building Blocks: A Women's Aid Guide to Running Refuges and Support Services.* Bristol: Women's Aid Federation of England.

Ungerson, C. (ed.) (1985) *Women and Social Policy.* London: Macmillan.

Walby, S. (2004) *The Cost of Domestic Violence.* London: Department of Trade and Industry.

Walby, S. and Allen, J. (2004) *Domestic Violence, Sexual Assault and Stalking: Findings from the British Crime Survey.* Home Office Research Study no. 276, London: Home Office.

Walker, L. (1984) *The Battered Woman Syndrome.* New York: Springer.

Walker, L. (1993) 'The battered woman syndrome is a psychological consequence of abuse.' In R. Gelles and D. Loseke (eds) *Current Controversies on Family Violence.* London: Sage.

Whalen, M. (1996) *Counselling to End Violence against Women: A Subversive Model.* London: Sage.

Williamson, E. (1999) 'Caught in contradictions.' In J. Radford, M. Friedberg and L. Harne (eds) *Women, Violence and Strategies for Action.* Maidenhead: Open University Press.

Worden, J.W. (1991) *Grief Counselling and Grief Therapy: A Handbook for the Mental Health Practitioner.* London: Routledge.

Yearnshaw, S. (1997) 'Police practice.' In S. Bewley, J. Friend and G. Mezey (eds) *Violence against Women.* London: Royal College of Obstetricians and Gynaecologists.

Subject Index

Author Index